Henry Meen

The Spirit of the nation

Ballads and songs

Henry Meen

The Spirit of the nation
Ballads and songs

ISBN/EAN: 9783742828729

Manufactured in Europe, USA, Canada, Australia, Japa

Cover: Foto ©Angelika Wolter / pixelio.de

Manufactured and distributed by brebook publishing software (www.brebook.com)

Henry Meen

The Spirit of the nation

THE
SPIRIT OF THE NATION;

OR,

BALLADS AND SONGS

BY

THE WRITERS OF "THE NATION."

CONTAINING ALL THE SONGS AND BALLADS FORMERLY
PUBLISHED IN TWO PARTS.

FIFTY-FIRST EDITION.

BOSTON COLLEGE LIBRARY
CHESTNUT HILL, MASS.

DUBLIN:
JAMES DUFFY & SONS, 15 WELLINGTON QUAY,
AND 1A PATERNOSTER ROW, LONDON.
1882.

ADVERTISEMENT TO THE FIFTIETH EDITION.

A New Edition of the "SPIRIT OF THE NATION" has been long called for, and is here presented in a clear, bold type. The old stereo plates, from which over one hundred thousand impressions had been printed, had got so completely worn out under the press, that copies printed from them were imperfect, and it became necessary to print a new edition in a style worthy of a work, the reputation of which has steadily risen with each succeeding generation, not only at home, but in England and America. Francis Jeffrey and Miss Mitford in England, and Longfellow in America, have written and spoken of some of the poems with enthusiasm; and a new demand for them has grown up in both countries.

The Present Edition is not a mere reprint of the two parts published in 1843. With all that is worth preserving in them, it unites the additional poems in the expensive quarto published in 1845, under the title of "Songs and Ballads by the Writers of THE NATION."

CONTENTS.

Names of Poems.	Authors' Names.	Page.
Adieu to Innisfail,	R. D. Williams,	63
Aid yourselves and God will aid you,	Sliabh Cuilinn,	171
Advance,	D. F. M'Carthy,	204
Annie, Dear,	Thomas Davis,	127
Anti-Irish Irishman,	Hugh Harkin,	253
Appeal, An,		53
Arms of Eighty-two,	M. J. Barry,	250
Ballad of Freedom,	Thomas Davis,	113
Battle of Beal-an-atha-Buidhe,	William Drennan,	44
Battle-Eve of the Brigade,	Thomas Davis,	108
Bide your Time,	M. J. Barry,	78
Bishop of Ross,	Dr. Madden,	190
Boatman of Kinsale,	Thomas Davis,	189
Boyhood's Years,	Rev. C. Meehan,	65
Brothers, Arise,	G. S. Phillips,	224
Cate of Ceann-mare,	D. F. M'Carthy,	183
Cease to do Evil, Learn to do Well,	D. F. M'Carthy,	117
Clare's Dragoons,	Thomas Davis,	176
Day Dreamer,	Charles Gavan Duffy,	111
Dear Land,	Sliabh Cuilinn,	20
Dream of the Future,	D. F. M'Carthy,	122
Eire a Ruin,	Sliabh Cuilinn,	91
England's Ultimatum,	Sliabh Cuilinn,	213
Erin, our own little Isle,	Fermoy,	23
Exterminator's Song,	J. C. O'Callaghan,	125
Fag an Bealagh,	Charles Gavan Duffy,	9
Fail of the Leaves,	Rev. C. Meehan,	180
Father Mathew,		68
Fill high to-night,	William Mulchineck,	238
Fireside,	D. F. M'Carthy,	253
Fontenoy,	Thomas Davis,	215
Gael and the Green,	M. J. Barry,	40

CONTENTS.

Names of Poems.	Authors' Names.	Page.
Gathering of the Nation,	J. D. Frazer,	97
Geraldines,	Thomas Davis,	98
Green above the Red,	Thomas Davis,	157
Green Flag,	M. J. Barry,	147
Health, A,	J. D. Frazer,	198
Highway for Freedom,	Clarence Mangan,	202
Hymn of Freedom,	M. J. Barry,	103
Inis-Eoghain,	Charles Gavan Duffy,	82
Irish Arms Bill,	William Drennan,	208
Irish Reaper's Harvest Hymn,	John Keegan,	62
Irish War Song,	Edward Walsh,	35
Israelite Leader,	A———,	149
Kate of Araglen,	Denny Lane,	163
Lament of Grainne Maol,	Hugh Harkin,	242
Lament for Owen Roe O'Neill,	Thomas Davis,	11
Lament for the Milesians,	Thomas Davis,	140
Lay Sermon,	Charles Gavan Duffy,	186
Lion and Serpent,	R. D. Williams,	53
Lost Path,	Thomas Davis,	71
Love's Longings,	Thomas Davis,	246
Memory of the Dead,		41
Men of Tipperary,	Thomas Davis,	61
Munster,	Sliabh Cuilinn,	142
Munster War Song,	R. D. Williams,	51
Muster of the North,	Charles Gavan Duffy,	28
My Grave,	Thomas Davis,	210
My Land,	Thomas Davis,	138
Nation's First Number,	Clarence Mangan,	17
New Year's Song,	D. F. M'Carthy,	129
O'Connell,	Astrea,	14
O'Donnell abu,	M. J. M'Cann,	235
Oh! for a Steed,	Thomas Davis,	131
Orange and Green will carry the day,	Thomas Davis,	199
Our Course,	J. D. Frazer,	219
Our Own again,	Thomas Davis,	193
Ourselves Alone,	Sliabh Cuilinn,	56
Paddies Evermore,	Sliabh Cuilinn,	84
Past and Present,	Sliabh Cuilinn,	248
Patience,	Spartacus,	155
Patriot Brave,	R. D. Williams,	179
Patriot's Bride,	Charles Gavan Duffy,	74
Patriot's Haunts,	William Mulchineck,	196
Peasant Girls,		108

CONTENTS.

Names of Poems.	Authors' Names.	Page.
Pillar Towers of Ireland,	D. F. M'Carthy,	165
Price of Freedom,	D. F. M'Carthy,	79
Rally for Ireland,	Thomas Davis,	88
Recruiting Song of the Irish Brigade,	Maurice O'Connell,	152
Right Road,	Thomas Davis,	87
Saxon Shilling,	K. T. Buggy,	54
Slaves' Bill,	William Drennan,	209
Shan Van Vacht,	Michael Doheny,	95
Song for July the 12th, 1843,	J. D. Frazer,	86
Song of the Penal Days,	Edward Walsh,	70
Song of the Volunteers of 1782,	Thomas Davis,	38
Songs of the Nation,	Edward Walsh,	110
Sonnet,	E. N. Shannon,	22
Stand Together,	Beta,	26
Steady,	R. D. Williams,	231
Step Together,	M. J. Barry,	154
Sword, The,	M. J. Barry,	119
True Irish King,	Thomas Davis,	144
Tone's Grave,	Thomas Davis,	93
Tyrol and Ireland,	Theta,	25
Union, The,	Sliabh Cuillin,	105
Up for the Green,	Fermoy,	135
Victor's Burial,	Thomas Davis,	222
Voice and Pen,	D. F. M'Carthy,	133
Voice of Labor,	Charles Gavan Duffy,	47
Vow of Tipperary,	Thomas Davis,	211
Was It a Dream,	John O'Connell,	72
Watch and Wait,	Charles Gavan Duffy,	174
Welcome,	Thomas Davis,	140
West's Asleep,	Thomas Davis,	60
Wexford Massacre,	M. J. Barry,	252
What's my Thought like,	John O'Connell,	227
Why, Gentles, why,	L. N. F.	162
Wild Geese,	M. J. Barry,	169

THE SPIRIT OF THE NATION.

FAG AN BEALACH.*

[To make the general tone and some of the allusions in this song intelligible, we should, perhaps, mention that it was written in October, 1842, when the hope and spirits of the people were low; and published in the third number of the *Nation*, as the Charter-song of the contributors. It was supposed to be first sung, as it actually was, at one of their weekly suppers.]

BY CHARLES GAVAN DUFFY.

I.

" HOPE no more for fatherland,
   All its ranks are thinned or broken ;"
Long a base and coward band
   Recreant words like these have spoken :
   But WE preach a land awoken ;
Fatherland is true and tried
   As your fears are false and hollow ;
Slaves and dastards, stand aside—
   Knaves and traitors, *Fag an Bealach!*

---

* *Fag an Bealach,* "Clear the road," or, as it is vulgarly spelt, *Paugh a Ballagh,* was the cry with which the clans of Connaught and Munster used in faction fights to come through a fair with high hearts and smashing shillelahs. The regiments raised in the South and West took their old shout with them to the Continent. The 87th, or Royal Irish

II.

Know, ye suffering brethren ours,
    Might is strong, but Right is stronger;
Saxon wiles or Saxon pow'rs
    Can enslave our land no longer
    Than your own dissensions wrong her;
Be ye one in might and mind—
    Quit the mire where cravens wallow—
And your foes shall flee like wind
    From your fearless *Fag an Bealach!*

III.

Thus the mighty multitude
    Speak in accents hoarse with sorrow:
" We are fallen, but unsubdued;
    Show us whence we hope may borrow,
    And we'll fight your fight to-morrow.
Be but cautious, true, and brave,
    Where you lead us we will follow;
Hill and valley, rock and wave,
    Soon shall hear our *Fag an Bealach!*"

IV.

Fling our banner to the wind,
    Studded o'er with names of glory;

Fusileers, from their use of it, went generally by the name of "The Faugh a Ballagh Boys." "Nothing," says Napier, in his *History of the Peninsular War*—"nothing so startled the French soldiery as the wild yell with which the Irish regiments sprang to the charge;" and never was that haughty and intolerant shout raised in battle, but a charge swift as thought, and fatal as flame, came with it, like a rushing incarnation of *Fag an Bealach!*

Worth, and wit, and might, and mind,
　Poet young, and patriot hoary,
　Long shall make it shine in story.
Close your ranks—the moment's come—
　NOW, ye men of Ireland! follow;
Friends of Freedom, charge them home—
　Foes of Freedom, *Fag an Bealach!*

LAMENT FOR THE DEATH OF EOGHAN RUADH O'NEILL,

COMMONLY CALLED OWEN ROE O'NEIL.

[This striking and dramatic ballad was the *first* written by Thomas Davis. Before the publication of the first number of the *Nation*, Davis, Dillon, and Duffy agreed to attempt political ballads, on which they had great reliance for raising the spirit of the country: to their next meeting Davis brought the "Lament for Owen Roe," and "The Men of Tipperary."]

BY THOMAS DAVIS.

Time—10th November, 1649. Scene—Ormond's camp. Co. Waterford. Speakers—a veteran of Owen O'Neil's clan, and one of the horsemen just arrived with an account of his death.

I.

"Did they dare, did they dare, to slay Owen Roe O'Neil?"
"Yes, they slew with poison him they feared to meet with steel."
"May God wither up their hearts! May their blood cease to flow!
May they walk in living death, who poisoned Owen Roe!

II.

"Though it break my heart to hear, say again the
    bitter words."
"From Derry, against Cromwell, he marched to
    measure swords;
But the weapon of the Saxon met him on his way,
And he died at Cloc Uactair, upon Saint Leonard's
    Day."

III.

"Wail, wail ye for the Mighty One! Wail, wail
    ye for the Dead!
Quench the hearth, and hold the breath—with
    ashes strew the head!
How tenderly we loved him! How deeply we
    deplore!
Holy Saviour! but to think we shall never see him
    more!

IV.

"Sagest in the council was he, kindest in the hall:
Sure we never won a battle—'twas Owen won
    them all.
Had he lived, had he lived, our dear country had
    been free;
But he's dead, but he's **dead**, and 'tis slaves we'll
    ever be.

V.

"O'Farrell and Clanrickarde, Preston and Red
    Hugh,
Audley and MacMahon, ye are valiant, wise, and
    true ;
But what—what are ye all to our darling who is
    gone?
The rudder of our ship was he—our castle's
    corner-stone!

VI.

" Wail, wail him through the island! Weep, weep
    for our pride!
Would that on the battle-field our gallant chief
    had died!
Weep the victor of Beinn Burb—weep him, young
    men and old!
Weep for him, ye women—your Beautiful lies
    cold!

VII.

We thought you would not die—we were sure
    you would not go,
And leave us in our utmost need to Cromwell's
    cruel blow—
Sheep without a shepherd, when the snow shuts
    out the sky—
Oh! why did you leave us, Owen? why did you
    die?

VIII.

"Soft as woman's was your voice, O'Neil! bright
    was your eye!
Oh! why did you leave us, Owen? why did
    you die?
Your troubles are all over—you're at rest with
    God on high;
But we're slaves, and we're orphans, Owen!—why
    did you die?"

O'CONNELL.

I.

I saw him at the hour of pray'r, when morning's
    earliest dawn
Was breaking o'er the mountain-tops—o'er grassy
    dell and lawn—
When the parting shades of night had fled—when
    moon and stars were gone,
Before a high and gorgeous shrine the chieftain
    kneeled alone.
His hands were clasped upon his breast, his eye
    was raised above—
I heard those full and solemn tones in words of
    faith and love;
He prayed that those who wronged him might for
    ever be forgiven;
Oh! who would say such prayers as *these* are not
    received in heaven?

II.

I saw him next amid the best and noblest of our
  isle—
There was the same majestic form, the same heart-
  kindling smile!
But grief was on that princely brow—for others
  still he mourned—
He gazed upon poor, fettered slaves, and his heart
  within him burned;
And he vowed before the captive's God to break
  the captive's chain—
To bind the broken heart, and set the bondsman
  free again;   [need,
And fit he was our chief to be, in triumph or in
Who never wronged his deadliest foe in thought,
  or word, or deed.

III.

I saw him when the light of eve had faded from
  the west—
Beside the hearth that old man sat, by infant forms
  caressed;
One hand was gently laid upon his grandchild's
  clustering hair,
The other, raised to heaven, invoked a blessing
  and a pray'r!
And woman's lips were heard to breathe a high
  and glorious strain—
Those songs of old, that haunt us still, and ever
  will remain

Within the heart like treasured gems—that bring
    from mem'ry's cell
Thoughts of our youthful days, and friends that
    we have loved so well!

IV.

I saw that eagle glance again—the brow was
    marked with care,
Though rich and regal are the robes the Nation's
    chief doth wear;*
And many an eye now quailed with shame, and
    many a cheek now glowed,
As he paid them back with words of love for
    every curse bestowed.
I thought of his unceasing care, his never-ending
    zeal;
I heard the watchword burst from all—the
    gathering cry—*Repeal!*
And, as his eyes were raised to heaven—from
    whence his mission came—
He stood, amid the thousands there, a monarch, save in
    name.

ASTREA.

---

* Written during his mayoralty.

THE NATION'S FIRST NUMBER.

BY CLARENCE MANGAN.
Air—"*Rory O'More.*"

I.

'Tis a great day, and glorious, O Public! for you—
This October Fifteenth, Eighteen Forty and Two!
For on this day of days, lo! THE NATION came
    forth,
To commence its career of Wit, Wisdom, and
    Worth—
To give genius its due—to do battle with wrong—
And achieve things undreamed of as yet, save in
    song.
Then arise! fling aside your dark mantle of slumber,
And welcome in chorus THE NATION'S FIRST
    NUMBER.

II.

Here we are, thanks to heaven! in an epoch when
    Mind
Is unfettering our captives, and couching our blind;
And the Press, with its thunders, keeps marring
    the mirth
Of those tyrants and bigots that curse our fair earth.
Be it ours to stand forth and contend in the van
Of truth's legions for freedom, that birthright of
    man:

B

Shaking off the dull cobwebs that else might
    encumber
Our weapon—the pen—in THE NATION'S FIRST
    NUMBER.

III.

We announce a New Era—be this our first news—
When the serf-grinding landlords shall shake in
    their shoes,
While the ark of a bloodless yet mighty Reform
Shall emerge from the flood of the popular storm!
Well we know how the lickspittle panders to pow'r
Feel and fear the approach of that death-dealing
    hour;
But we toss these aside—such vile, vagabond lumber
Are but just worth a groan from THE NATION'S
    FIRST NUMBER.

IV.

Though we take not for motto, *Nul n'a de l'esprit*
(As they once did in Paris) *hors nos bons amis,*
We may boast that for first-rate endowments our
    band
Forms a phalanx unmatched *in*—or *out* of—the land,
Poets, Patriots, Linguists, with reading like Parr's—
Critics keener than sabres—Wits brighter than
    stars,
And Reasoners as cool as the coolest cucumber,
Form the host that shine out in THE NATION'S
    FIRST NUMBER.

V.

We shall sketch living manners and men, in a
 style
That will scarcely be sneezed at, we guess, for a
 while ;
Build up stories as fast as of yore Mother Bunch ;
And for fun of all twists take the shine out of
 " PUNCH ;"
Thus our Wisdom and Quizdom will finely agree,
Very much, Public dear, we conceive, as you see,
Do the lights and the shades that illume and
 adumber
Each beautiful page in THE NATION'S FIRST
 NUMBER.

VI.

A word more. TO OLD IRELAND our first love is
 given,
Still our friendship hath arms for all lands under
 heaven.
WE ARE IRISH—we vaunt it—all o'er and all out ;
But we wish not that England shall "sneak up the
 spout !"
Then, O Public ! here, there, and elsewhere through
 the world,
Wheresoe'er TRUTH'S and LIBERTY'S flags are un-
 furled,
From the Suir to the Rhine, from the Boyne to
 the Humber,
Raise one shout of applause for THE NATION'S
 FIRST NUMBER.

DEAR LAND.

I.

When comes the day all hearts to weigh,
    If staunch they be, or vile,
Shall we forget the sacred debt
    We owe our mother isle?
My native heath is brown beneath,
    My native waters blue;
But crimson red o'er both shall spread,
    Ere I am false to you,
                  Dear land!
  Ere I am false to you.

II.

When I behold your mountains bold—
    Your noble lakes and streams—
A mingled tide of grief and pride
    Within my bosom teems.
I think of all your long, dark thrall—
    Your martyrs brave and true;
And dash apart the tears that start—
    We must not *weep* for you,
                  Dear land!
  We must not *weep* for you.

III.

My grandsire died, his home beside ;
   They seized and hanged him there ;
His only crime, in evil time
   Your hallowed green to wear.
Across the main his brothers twain
   Were sent to pine and rue ;
And still they turned with hearts that burned
   In hopeless love to you,
               Dear land !
   In hopeless love to you.

IV.

My boyish ear still clung to hear
   Of Erin's pride of yore,
Ere Norman foot had dared pollute
   Her independent shore ;
Of chiefs, long dead, who rose to head
   Some gallant patriot few ;
Till all my aim on earth became
   To strike one blow for you,
               Dear land !
   To strike one blow for you !

V.

What path is best your rights to wrest
   Let other heads divine ;
By work or word, with voice or sword,
   To follow them be mine.

The breast that zeal and hatred steel
  No terrors can subdue;
If death should come, that martyrdom
  Were sweet endured for you,
            Dear land!
  Were sweet endured for you.

SLIABH CUILINN.

SONNET.

BY F. N. SHANNON,

Translator of Dante, Author of "Tales Old and New."

In fair, delightful Cyprus, by the main,
  A lofty, royal seat, Love's dwelling stands;
  Thither I went, and gave into his hands
An humble scroll, his clemency to gain.
"Sire," said the writing, "Thyrsis, who in pain
  Has served thee hitherto, this boon demands—
His freedom; neither should his suit be vain,
  After six lustres' service in thy bands."
He took the scroll, and seemed to pore thereon;
  But he was blind, and could not read the case.
    Seeming to feel his grievous want full sore—
Wherefore, with stern and frowning air, anon
  He said, and flung my writing in my face:
    "Give it to DEATH—we two will talk it o'er."

ERIN—*OUR OWN* LITTLE ISLE.

Air—"*The Caravat Jig.*"

I.

O Irishmen! never forget
  'Tis a *foreigner's farm*—your own little isle;
O Irishmen! when will you get
  Some *life* in your hearts for your poor little isle?
    Yes! yes!—we've a dear little spot of it!
     Oh! yes!—a sweet little isle!
    Yes! yes!—if Irishmen thought of it,
     'Twould be a dear little, sweet little isle!

II.

Then, come on and rise—ev'ry man of you;
  Now is the time for a stir to be made;
Ho! Pat! who made such a lamb of you?
  Life to your soul, boy, and strength to your blade!
    Yes! yes!—a dear little spot of it!
     Oh! yes!—a sweet little isle!
    Yes! yes!—if Irishmen thought of it,
     Erin once more is *our own* little isle!

III.

Rise heartily! shoulder to shoulder,
  We'll show 'em strength with good humour
    go leor!
Rise! rise! show each foreign beholder
  We've *not* lost our love to thee, Erin *a stóir!*

For, oh! yes!—'tis a dear little spot of it!
   Yes! yes!—a sweet little isle!
Yes! yes!—the Irish *have* thought of it;
   Erin for ever—*our own* little isle!

IV.

Never forget what your forefathers fought for, O!
   When, with "O'Neill!" or "O'Donnell aboo!"
Sassenaghs ev'rywhere sunk in the slaughter, O!
   Vengeance for insult, dear Erin, to you!
     For, oh! yes!—a dear little spot of it!
       Yes! yes!—a sweet little isle;
     Yes! yes!—if Irishmen thought of it,
       Erin once more is *our own* little isle!

V.

Yes, we *have* strength to make Irishmen free again;
   Only UNITE—and we'll conquer our foe;
And never on earth shall a foreigner see again
   Erin a province—though lately so low.
     For, oh! yes!—we've a dear little spot of it!
       Yes! yes!—a sweet little isle!
     Yes! yes!—the Irish *have* thought of it;
       Erin *for ever*—OUR OWN little isle!

                              FERMOY.

TYROL AND IRELAND.

"Ye gather three ears of corn, and they take two out of three. Are ye contented? are ye happy? But there is a Providence above, and there are angels; and when we seek to right ourselves, they will assist us."— *Speech of Hofer to the Tyrolese*, 1809.

I.

And Hofer roused Tyrol for this,
   Made Winschgau red with blood,
Thal Botzen's peasants ranged in arms,
   And Inspruck's fire withstood.
For this! for this! that but a third
   The hind his own could call,
When Passyer gathered in her sheaves;
   Why, *ye* are robbed of all.

II.

Up rose the hardy mountaineers,
   And crushed Bavaria's horse,
I' th' name of Father and of Son,*
   For *this* without remorse.
Great Heaven, for this! that Passyer's swains
   Of half their store were rest;
Why, clods of senseless clay! to you
   Not even a sheaf is left!

---

* "The Bavarian vanguard, composed of 4,000 men, advanced into the defile; and when they had reached midway, the mountaineers hurled down upon their heads huge rocks, which they had rolled to the verge of the precipice, in the name of the Father, the Son, and the Holy Ghost."— *Histoire des Tyroliens*.

III.

'Midst plenty gushing round, ye starve—
    'Midst blessings, crawl accurst—
And hoard for your land-cormorants all,
    Deep gorging till they burst!
Still, still they spurn you with contempt,
    Deride your pangs with scorn,
Still bid you bite the dust, for churls
    And villains basely born!

IV.

O idiots! feel ye not the lash?
    The fangs that clutch at gold?
From rogues so insolent what hope
    Of mercy do ye hold?
The pallid millions kneel for food;
    The lordling locks his store.
Hath earth, alas! but one Tyrol,
    And not a Hofer more.

THETA.

STAND TOGETHER.

I.

STAND together, brothers all!
    Stand together, stand together!
To live or die, to rise or fall,
    Stand together, stand together!

Old Erin proudly lifts her head—
Of many tears the last is shed;
Oh! *for* the living—*by* the dead!
    Stand together, true together!

II.

Stand together, brothers all!
    Close together, close together!
Be Ireland's might a brazen wall—
    Close up together, tight together!
Peace! no noise!—but, hand in hand,
Let calm resolve pervade your band,
And wait, till nature's God command—
    Then help each other, help each other.

III.

Stand together, brothers all!
    Proud together, bold together!
From Kerry's cliffs to Donegal,
    Bound in heart and soul together!
Unroll the sunburst! who'll defend
Old Erin's banner is a friend;
One foe is ours—oh! blend, boys, blend
    Hands together—hearts together!

IV.

Stand together, brothers all!
    Wait together, watch together!
See, America and Gaul
    Look on together, both together!

Keen impatience in each eye;
Yet on "ourselves" do we rely—
"Ourselves alone" our rallying cry!
And "stand together, strike together!"
BETA.

THE MUSTER OF THE NORTH.
A.D. 1641.
BY CHARLES GAVAN DUFFY.

[We deny and have always denied the alleged massacre of 1641. But that the people rose under their chiefs, seized the English towns and expelled the English settlers, and in doing so committed many excesses, is undeniable—as is equally the desperate provocation. The ballad here printed is not meant as an apology for these excesses, which we condemn and lament, but as a true representation of the feelings of the insurgents in the first madness of success.]

I.

Joy! joy! the day is come at last, the day of hope and pride—
And see! our crackling bonfires light old Bann's rejoicing tide,
And gladsome bell and bugle-horn from Newry's captured towers,
Hark! how they tell the Saxon swine, this land is ours, is OURS.

II.

Glory to God! my eyes have seen the ransomed fields of Down.
My ears have drunk the joyful news, "Stout Phelim hath his own."

Oh! may they see and hear no more, oh! may they
    rot to clay,
When they forget to triumph in the conquest of
    to-day.

III.

Now, now we'll teach the shameless Scot to purge
    his thievish maw ;
Now, now the Court may fall to pray, for Justice
    is the Law ;
Now shall the Undertaker* square, for once, his
    loose accounts—
We'll strike, brave boys, a fair result, from all his
    false amounts.

IV.

Come, trample down their robber rule, and smite
    its venal spawn,
Their foreign laws, their foreign church, their
    ermine and their lawn,
With all the specious fry of fraud that robbed us
    of our own ;
And plant our ancient laws again beneath our
    lineal throne.

V.

Our standard flies o'er fifty towers, o'er twice ten
    thousand men ;
Down have we plucked the pirate Red, never to
    rise again ;

---

* The Scotch and English adventurers planted in Ulster by James I.
were called Undertakers.

The Green alone shall stream above our native
　　field and flood—
The spotless Green, save where its folds are gemmed
　　with Saxon blood!

VI.

Pity!* no, no, you dare not, priest—not you, our
　　father, dare
Preach to us now that godless creed—the mur-
　　derer's blood to spare;
To spare his blood, while tombless still our slaugh-
　　tered kin implore
"Graves and revenge" from Gobbin cliffs and
　　Carrick's bloody shore!†

VII.

Pity!—could we "forget, forgive," if we were
　　clods of clay,
Our martyred priests, our banished chiefs, our race
　　in dark decay,
And, worse than all—you know it, priest—the
　　daughters of our land
With wrongs we blushed to name until the sword
　　was in our hand?

---

* Leland, the Protestant historian, states that the Catholic priests
"*labored zealously to moderate the excesses of war*," and frequently
protected the English by concealing them in their places of worship and
even under their altars.

† The scene of the massacre of the unoffending inhabitants of Island
Magee by the garrison of Carrickfergus.

VIII.

Pity! well, if you needs must whine, let pity have its way,
Pity for all our comrades true, far from our side to-day:
The prison-bound who rot in chains, the faithful dead who poured
Their blood 'neath Temple's lawless axe or Parson's ruffian sword.

IX.

They smote us with the swearer's oath, and with the murderer's knife;
We in the open field will fight fairly for land and life;
But, by the dead and all their wrongs, and by our hopes to-day,
One of us twain shall fight their last, or be it we or they.

X.

They banned our faith, they banned our lives, they trod us into earth,
Until our very patience stirred their bitter hearts to mirth.
Even this great flame that wraps them now, not *we* but *they* have bred:
Yes, this is their own work; and now their work be on their head!

XI.

Nay, father, tell us not of help from Leinster's
  Norman peers,
If we shall shape our holy cause to match their
  selfish fears—
Helpless and hopeless be their cause who brook a
  vain delay!
Our ship is launched, our flag's afloat, whether they
  come or stay.

XII.

Let silken Howth and savage Slane still kiss their
  tyrant's rod,
And pale Dunsany still prefer his master to his
  God;
Little we'd miss their fathers' sons, the Marchmen
  of the Pale,
If Irish hearts and Irish hands had Spanish blade
  and mail!

XIII.

Then, let them stay to bow and fawn, or fight with
  cunning words;
I fear me more their courtly arts than England's
  hireling swords;
Nathless their creed, they hate us still, as the
  despoiler hates;
Could they love us, and love their prey, our kins-
  men's lost estates?

XIV.

Our rude array's a jagged rock to smash the spoiler's
    pow'r,
Or, need we aid, His aid we have who doomed this
    gracious hour;
Of yore He led His Hebrew host to peace through
    strife and pain,
And us he leads the self-same path, the self-same
    goal to gain.

XV.

Down from the sacred hills whereon a saint* com-
    muned with God,
Up from the vale where Bagenal's blood manured
    the reeking sod,
Out from the stately woods of Truagh, M'Kenna's
    plundered home,
Like Malin's waves, as fierce and fast, our faithful
    clansmen come.

XVI.

Then, brethren, *on!* O'Neill's dear shade would
    frown to see you pause—
Our banished Hugh, our martyred Hugh, is watch-
    ing o'er your cause—
His generous error lost the land—he deemed the
    Norman true;
Oh, forward! friends, it must not lose the land
    again in you!

---

* St. Patrick, whose favorite retreat was Lecale, in the Co. Down.

NOTE ON "THE MUSTER OF THE NORTH."

The *Times* newspaper, in the absence of any topic of public interest, having made this ballad the subject of a leading article, in which extravagant praise of its literary merits was joined with an equally extravagant misrepresentation of its object and tendency, it had the hard fortune to run the gauntlet of all the Tory journals in the empire, and to become the best abused ballad in existence. It was described as the *Rosg-Cata* of a new rebellion—as a deliberate attempt to revive the jealousies of the bill of settlement; and the organ of the General Assembly of Ulster coolly proclaimed the writer to be a man with the intellect, but also with the heart, of Satan! Under these circumstances I should not have permitted its insertion in the present edition, had I not feared that omitting it might be interpreted into an admission of charges, than which nothing can possibly be more false or ludicrous. In writing it, I had simply in view to produce—what it will not be denied an historical ballad ought to be—a picture of the *actual feelings* of the times in which the scene is laid; and the sentiments are certainly not more violent than the great masters of ballad poetry—Scott, for example, in his "Glencoe"—have put into the mouths of injured men. Possibly the prejudice in the present case arose from overlooking the fact that these sentiments are attributed to men who had been plundered of two provinces by a false king, imprisoned for returning conscientious verdicts, robbed by enormous fines, persecuted for the exercise of their religion, and subject to a long series of tyrannies, which historians, without exception, have described as cruel and infamous. To make these men talk coolly, and exhibit all the horror of spilling one drop of human blood into which O'Connell has trained this generation, would be very much on a par, in point of sense and propriety, with the old stage custom of dressing Richard III. in the uniform of the Coldstream Guards. So little intention, however, was there to make it available to any political purpose, that there is not a single allusion in the poem that was not suggested by the circumstances of the period; while some of them would be quite inapplicable to any other time, especially to the present (1844).

IRISH WAR-SONG.

BY EDWARD WALSH.

Air—"*The world's turned upside down.*"

Bright sun! before whose glorious ray
    Our pagan fathers bent the knee;
Whose pillar-altars yet can say
    When time was young our sires were free;
Who seest how fallen their offspring be,
    Our matrons' tears, our patriots' gore;
We swear, before high heaven and thee,
    The Saxon holds us slaves no more!

Our sunburst on the Roman foe
    Flashed vengeance once in foreign field;
On Clontarf's plain lay scathed low
    What power the sea-kings fierce could wield;
Beinn Burb might say whose cloven shield
    'Neath bloody hoofs was trampled o'er;
And, by these memories high, we yield
    Our limbs to Saxon chains no more!

The *clairseach* wild, whose trembling string
    Had long the "song of sorrow" spoke,
Shall bid the wild *Rosg-Cata** sing
    The curse and crime of Saxon yoke.

* Literally the "Eye of Battle"— the war-song of the bards.

And, by each heart his bondage broke—
    Each exile's sigh on distant shore—
Each martyr 'neath the headsman's stroke—
    The Saxon holds us slaves no more!

Send the loud war-cry o'er the main—
    Your sunburst to the breezes spread:
That *slogan* rends the heaven in twain—
    The earth reels back beneath your tread.
Ye Saxon despots, hear, and dread!
    Your march o'er patriot hearts is o'er—
That shout hath told, that tramp hath said,
    Our country's sons are slaves no more!

SONG FOR JULY 12TH, 1843.

BY J. D. FRASER.

Air—"*Boyne Water.*"

Come—pledge again thy heart and hand—
    One grasp that ne'er shall sever;
Our watchword be—"Our native land"—
    Our motto—"Love for ever."
And let the Orange lily be
    Thy badge, my patriot brother—
The everlasting Green for *me*;
    And we for one another.

THE SPIRIT OF THE NATION.

Behold how green the gallant stem
    On which the flower is blowing;
How in one heavenly breeze and beam
    Both flower and stem are glowing.
The same good soil, sustaining both,
    Makes both united flourish;
But cannot give the Orange growth,
    And cease the Green to nourish.

Yea, more—the hand that plucks the flow'r
    Will vainly strive to cherish;
The stem blooms on—but in that hour
    The flower begins to perish.
Regard them, then, of equal worth
    While lasts their genial weather;
The time's at hand when into earth
    The two shall sink together.

Ev'n thus be, in our country's cause,
    Our party feelings blended;
Till lasting peace, from equal laws,
    On both shall have descended.
Till then the Orange lily be
    Thy badge, my patriot brother—
The everlasting Green for *me;*
    And—we for one another.

SONG OF THE VOLUNTEERS OF 1782.

BY THOMAS DAVIS.

AIR—"*Boyne Water.*"

Hurrah! 'tis done—our freedom's won—
   Hurrah for the Volunteers!
No laws we own, but those alone
   Of our Commons, King, and Peers.
The chain is broke—the Saxon yoke
   From off our neck is taken;
Ireland awoke—Dungannon spoke—
   With fear was England shaken.

When Grattan rose, none dared oppose
   The claim he made for freedom;
They knew our swords, to back his words,
   Were ready, did he need them.
Then let us raise, to Grattan's praise,
   A proud and joyous anthem;
And wealth, and grace, and length of days,
   May God in mercy grant him!

Bless Harry Flood, who nobly stood
   By us through gloomy years;
Bless Charlemont, the brave and good,
   The Chief of the Volunteers!

The North began, the North held on
    The strife for native land,
Till Ireland rose, and cowed her foes—
    God bless the Northern land!

And bless the men of patriot pen—
    Swift, Molyneux, and Lucas;
Bless sword and gun which "Free Trade" won;
    Bless God! who ne'er forsook us!
And long may last the friendship fast
    Which binds us all together;
While we agree, our foes shall flee
    Like clouds in stormy weather.

Remember still, through good and ill,
    How vain were prayers and tears—
How vain were words, till flashed the swords
    Of the Irish Volunteers.
By arms we've got the rights we sought
    Through long and wretched years:
Hurrah! 'tis done—our freedom's won—
    Hurrah for the Volunteers!

THE GAEL AND THE GREEN.

BY M. J. BARRY.

Air—"*One bumper at parting.*"

Come, fill every glass to o'erflowing,
　With wine, or *potheen* if you will,
Or, if any think these are too glowing,
　Let water replace them—but fill!
Oh! trust me, 'tis churlish and silly
　To ask how the bumper's filled up;
If the tide in the heart be not chilly,
　What matters the tide in the cup?
Oh! ne'er may that heart's tide ascending
　In shame on our foreheads be seen,
While it nobly can ebb in defending
　Our own glorious color—the Green!

In vain did oppression endeavor
　To trample that Green under foot;
The fair stem was broken, but never
　Could tyranny reach to its root
Then come, and around it let's rally,
　And guard it henceforward like men!
Oh! soon shall each mountain and valley
　Glow bright with its verdure again.

Meanwhile, fill each glass to the brim, boys,
   With water, with wine, or *potheen*,
And on each let the honest wish swim, boys—
   Long flourish the Gael and the Green!

Here, under our host's gay dominion,
   While gathered this table around,
What varying shades of opinion
   In one happy circle are found!
What opposite creeds come together!
   How mingle North, South, East, and West!
Yet who minds the diff'rence a feather?—
   Each strives to love Erin the best.
Oh! soon through our beautiful island
   May union as blessed be seen,
While floats o'er each valley and highland
   Our own glorious color—the Green!

THE MEMORY OF THE DEAD.*

Who fears to speak of Ninety-Eight?
   Who blushes at the name?
When cowards mock the patriot's fate,
   Who hangs his head for shame?

---

* The music to which this fine song is set will be found in the "Ballads and Songs by the Writers of the *Nation*, with original and ancient music." JAMES DUFFY, 1845.

He's all a knave or half a slave
    Who slights his country thus;
But a *true* man, like you, man,
    Will fill your glass with us.

We drink the memory of the brave,
    The faithful and the few—
Some lie far off beyond the wave,
    Some sleep in Ireland, too;
All, all are gone—but still lives on
    The fame of those who died;
All true men, like you, men,
    Remember them with pride.

Some on the shores of distant lands
    Their weary hearts have laid,
And by the stranger's heedless hands
    Their lonely graves were made;
But, though their clay be far away
    Beyond the Atlantic foam,
In true men, like you, men,
    Their spirit's still at home.

The dust of some is Irish earth;
    Among their own they rest;
And the same land that gave them birth
    Has caught them to her breast;

And we will pray that from their clay
    Full many a race may start
Of true men, like you, men,
    To act as brave a part.

They rose in dark and evil days
    To right their native land;
They kindled here a living blaze
    That nothing shall withstand.
Alas! that Might can vanquish Right—
    They fell, and passed away;
But true men, like you, men,
    Are plenty here to-day.

Then here's their memory—may it be
    For us a guiding light,
To cheer our strife for liberty,
    And teach us to unite!
Through good and ill, be Ireland's still,
    Though sad as theirs your fate;
And true men, be you, men,
    Like those of Ninety-Eight.

THE BATTLE OF BEAL-AN-ATHA-BUIDHE.

Won by the great Hugh O'Neill over Marshal Bagenal and the flower of Elizabeth's army, between Armagh and Blackwater Bridge, A.D. 1598.

BY WILLIAM DRENNAN.

By O'Neill close beleaguered, the spirits might droop
Of the Saxon three hundred shut up in their coop,
Till Bagenal drew forth his Toledo, and swore,
On the sword of a soldier, to succor Port Mor.

His veteran troops, in the foreign wars tried—
Their features how bronzed, and how haughty their stride—
Stept steadily on; it was thrilling to see
That thunder-cloud brooding o'er Beal-an-atha-buidhe.

The flash of their armor, inlaid with fine gold—
Gleaming matchlocks, and cannon that mutteringly rolled—
With the tramp and the clank of those stern cuirassiers
Dyed in blood of the Flemish and French cavaliers.

And are the mere Irish, with pikes and with darts,
With but glibb-covered heads, and but rib-guarded hearts—

Half-naked, half-fed, with few muskets, no guns—
The battle to dare against England's proud sons?

Poor bonnochts, and wild gallowglasses and
    kern*—
Let them war with rude brambles, sharp furze, and
    dry fern;
Wirrastrue† for their wives—for their babes *ochanie*,
If they wait for the Saxon at Beal-an-atha-buidhe.

Yet O'Neill standeth firm—few and brief his com-
    mands:
" Ye have hearts in your bosoms, and pikes in
    your hands;
Try how far you can push them, my children, at
    once;
Fag an bealach! and down with horse, foot, and
    great guns.

" They have gold and gay arms—they have biscuit
    and bread;
Now, sons of my soul, we'll be found and be fed;"
And he clutched his claymore, and, " Look yonder!"
    laughed he,
" What a grand commissariat for Beal-an-atha-
    buidhe!"

---

* *Buanadh*, a billeted soldier, from *buanacht*, quarterage. *Gallo-glach*, a heavy soldier. *Ceitheirn*, a band of light troops, plural of *Ceithearnaigh*.

† *Wirrastrue—A Mhuire as truagh*, O Mary, what sorrow!

Near the chief a grim tyke, an O'Shanaghan, stood;
His nostrils, dilated, seemed snuffing for blood;
Rough and ready to spring, like the wiry wolf-
    hound
Of Irenè—who, tossing his pike with a bound,

Cried, "My hand to the Sassanach! ne'er may I
    hurl
Another to earth if I call him a churl!
He finds me in clothing, in booty, and bread—
My chief, won't O'Shanaghan give him a bed?"

"Land of Owen aboo!" and the Irish rushed on—
The foe fired but one volley—their gunners are
    gone;
Before the bare bosoms the steel-coats have fled,
Or, despite casque and corselet, lie dying and dead.

And brave Harry Bagenal, he fell while he fought,
With many gay gallants—they slept as men
    ought,
Their faces to heaven; there were others, alack!
By pikes overtaken, and taken aback.

And my Irish got clothing, coin, colors, great
    store,
Arms, forage, and provender—plunder *go leor!*

They munched the white manchets—they champed
   the brown chine—
Fuillcluadh! for that day how the natives did
   dine!

The chieftain looked on, when O'Shanaghan rose,
And cried, "Hearken, O'Neill! I've a health to
   propose—
'To our Sassanach hosts!'" and all quaffed in huge
   glee,
With *Cead mile failte go* BEAL-AN-ATHA-BUIDHE!

THE VOICE OF LABOR.

A CHANT OF THE CITY MEETINGS, A.D. 1843.

BY CHARLES GAVAN DUFFY.

YE who despoil the sons of toil, saw ye this sight
   to-day,
When stalwart Trade, in long brigade, beyond a
   king's array,
Marched in the blessed light of heaven, beneath
   the open sky,
Strong in the might of sacred RIGHT, that none
   dare ask them why?
These are the slaves, the kneedy knaves, ye spit
   upon with scorn—
The spawn of earth, of nameless birth, and basely
   bred as born;

Yet know, ye soft and silken lords, were we the
    thing ye say,
Your broad domains, your coffered gains, your
    lives, were ours to-day.

Measure that rank from flank to flank—'tis fifty
    thousand strong;
And mark you here, in front and rear, brigades as
    deep and long;
And know that never blade of foe, or **Arran's**
    deadly breeze,
Tried, by assay of storm or fray, more dauntless
    hearts than these.
The sinewy smith, little he recks of his own child,
    the sword;
The men of gear, think you they fear *their* handi
    work—a lord?
And, undismayed, yon sons of trade might see the
    battle's front,
Who bravely bore, nor bowed before, the deadlier
    face of want.

What lack we here of show or form, that lure your
    slaves to death?
Not serried bands, nor sinewy hands, nor music's
    martial breath;   [endure,
And if we broke the bitter yoke our suppliant race
No robbers we—but chivalry—the Army of the
    Poor.

Shame on ye now, ye lorldly crew, that do your
　　betters wrong—
We are no base and braggart mob, but merciful
　　and strong.
Your henchmen vain, your vassal train, would fly
　　our first defiance ;
In us—in our strong, tranquil breasts—abides your
　　sole reliance.

Aye! keep them all, castle and hall, coffers and
　　costly jewels—
Keep your vile gain, and in its train the passions
　　that it fuels.　　　　　　　　　　　　[decayance ;
We envy not your lordly lot—its bloom or its
But ye *have* that we claim as ours—our right in
　　long abeyance—　　　　　　　　　　[freedom :
Leisure to live, leisure to love, leisure to taste our
Oh! suff'ring poor, oh! patient poor, how bitterly
　　you need them !　　　　　　　　　　[charter,
" Ever to moil, ever to toil," that is your social
And, city slave or peasant serf, the toiler is its
　　martyr.

Where Frank and Tuscan shed their sweat the
　　goodly crop is theirs ;
If Norway's toil make rich the soil, she eats the
　　fruit she rears ;
O'er Maine's green sward there rules no lord,
　　saving the Lord on high ;
But we are slaves in our own land—proud masters,
　　tell us why ?

　　　　　　　　　　　　　　　　　　　D

The German burgher and his men, brother with
    brothers live ;
While toil must wait without *your* gate what
    gracious crusts you give.
Long in your sight, for our own right, we've bent,
    and still we bend—
Why did we bow? why do we now?—proud
    masters, this must end.

Perish the past—a generous land is this fair land
    of ours,
And enmity may no man see between its towns
    and tow'rs.
Come, join our bands—here, take our hands—now
    shame on him that lingers!
Merchant or peer, you have no fear from labor's
    blistered fingers!
Come, join at last; perish the past—its traitors,
    its seceders—
Proud names and old, frank hearts and bold, come
    join, and be our leaders.
But know, ye lords, that be your swords with us
    or with our wronger,
Heaven be our guide, for we will bide this lot
    shame no longer!

THE MUNSTER WAR-SONG.
A.D. 1190.
BY R. D. WILLIAMS.

Air—"*And doth not a meeting.*"

[This ballad relates to the time when the Irish began to rally and unite against their invaders. The union was, alas! brief, but its effects were great. The troops of Connaught and Ulster, under Cathal Croibh-dearg (Cathal O'Connor of the Red Hand), defeated and slew Armoric St. Lawrence, and stripped De Courcy of half his conquests. But the ballad relates to Munster; and an extract from Moore's (the most accessible) book will show that there was solid ground for triumph: "Among the chiefs who agreed at this crisis to postpone their mutual feuds, and act in concert against the enemy, were O'Brian of Thomond, and Mac Carthy of Desmond, hereditary rulers of North and South Munster, and chiefs respectively of the two rival tribes, the Dalcassians and Eoganians. By a truce now formed between those princes, O'Brian was left free to direct his arms against the English; and having attacked their forces at Thurles, in Fogarty's country, gave them A COMPLETE OVERTHROW, putting to the sword, add the Munster annals, a great number of knights."—Moore's "History of Ireland," A.D. 1190.]

CAN the depths of the ocean afford you not graves,
That you come thus to perish afar o'er the waves—
To redden and swell the wild torrents that flow
Through the valley of vengeance, the dark Eatharlach ?*

The clangor of conflict o'erburthens the breeze,
From the stormy Sliabh Bloom to the stately Gailtees ;
Your caverns and torrents are purple with gore,
Sliabh na m-Ban,† Gleann Colaich, and sublime Gailtee Mor !

The sunburst that slumbered, embalmed in our tears,
Tipperary ! shall wave o'er thy tall mountaineers !
And the dark hill shall bristle with sabre and spear,
While one tyrant remains to forge manacles here.

* Aharlow Glen, county Tipperary. † Slievenamon.

The riderless war-steed careers o'er the plain
With a shaft in his flank and a blood-dripping mane,
His gallant breast labors, and glare his wild eyes!
He plunges in torture—falls—shivers—and dies.

Let the trumpets ring triumph! the tyrant is slain!
He reels o'er his charger deep-pierced through the
    brain;
And his myriads are flying like leaves on the gale—
But who shall escape from our hills with the tale?

For the arrows of vengeance are show'ring like rain,
And choke the strong rivers with islands of slain,
Till thy waves, "lordly Sionainn," all crimsonly flow,
Like the billows of hell, with the blood of the foe.

Ay! the foemen are flying, but vainly they fly—
Revenge with the fleetness of lightning can vie;
And the septs of the mountains spring up from
    each rock,
And rush down the ravines like wolves on the flock.

And who shall pass over the stormy Sliabh Bloom,
To tell the pale Saxon of tyranny's doom,
When, like tigers from ambush, our fierce moun-
    taineers
Leap along from the crags with their death-dealing
    spears?

They came with high boasting to bind us as slaves,
But the glen and the torrent have yawned on their
    graves:

From the gloomy Ard Fionnain to wild Teampoll
   Mor—*
From the Siur to the Sionainn—is red with their
   gore.

By the soul of Heremon! our warriors may smile,
To remember the march of the foe through our isle;
Their banners and harness were costly and gay,
And proudly they flashed in the summer sun's ray;

The hilts of their falchions were crusted with gold,
And the gems of their helmets were bright to be-
   hold;
By Saint Bride of Cildare! but they moved in fair
   show—
To gorge the young eagles of dark Eatharlach!

AN APPEAL.

ILL-FATED Erin! land of woe,
Still trodden down by foreign foe,
Why strike you not one final blow?

Long-suffering country! are not thine
For ambush meet the deep ravine,
And plains to form the embattled line?

The hardy Affghan, prompt and bold,
Unconquered in his mountain hold,
Bade Britain's bravest hearts wax cold.

* Ardfinan and Templemora.

Shall we, who boast a holier trust,
Whose stainless cause is pure and just—
Shall we still grovel in the dust?

Shall we, in banded millions strong,
Still bear the yoke we've borne too long?
Still crouch to insult, scorn, and wrong?

THE SAXON SHILLING.

BY K. T. BUGGY.

[Mr. Buggy was a native of Kilkenny, and for some time editor of the *Kilkenny Journal*. He was also a contributor to the *Citizen* Magazine, and an active agitator in the Repeal movement. He succeeded Mr. Gavan Duffy as editor of the *Belfast Vindicator* in 1843, when the latter established the *Nation*; and he died soon after in the midst of his labors.]

HARK! a martial sound is heard—
  The march of soldiers, fifing, drumming,
Eyes are staring, hearts are stirred—
  For bold recruits the brave are coming.
Ribands flaunting, feathers gay—
  The sounds and sights are surely thrilling!
Dazzled village youths to-day
  Will crowd to take the *Saxon Shilling!*

Ye, whose spirits will not bow
  In peace to parish tyrants longer—
Ye, who wear the villain brow—
  And ye, who pine in hopeless hunger—

Fools, without the brave man's faith—
　　All slaves and starvelings who are willing
To sell yourselves to shame and death—
　　Accept the fatal *Saxon Shilling.*

Ere you from your mountains go
　　To feel the scourge of foreign fever,
Swear to serve the faithless foe
　　That lures you from your land for ever!
Swear henceforth its tools to be—
　　To slaughter trained by ceaseless drilling—
Honor, home, and liberty
　　Abandoned for a *Saxon Shilling!*

Go—to find, 'mid crime and toil,
　　The doom to which such guilt is hurried!
Go—to leave on Indian soil
　　Your bones to bleach, accursed, unburied!
Go—to crush the just and brave,
　　Whose wrongs with wrath the world are filling!
Go—to slay each brother slave—
　　Or spurn the blood-stained *Saxon Shilling!*

Irish hearts! why should you bleed
　　To swell the tide of British glory—
Aiding despots in their need,
　　Who've changed our *green* so oft to *gory?*
None, save those who wish to see
　　The noblest killed, the meanest killing,
And true hearts severed from the free,
　　Will take again the *Saxon Shilling!*

Irish youths! reserve your strength
 Until an hour of glorious duty,
When freedom's smile shall cheer at length
 The land of bravery and beauty.
Bribes and threats, oh! heed no more—
 Let nought but JUSTICE make you willing
To leave your own dear island shore
 For those who send the *Saxon Shilling*.

OURSELVES ALONE.

THE work that should to-day be wrought,
 Defer not till to-morrow;
The help that should within be sought,
 Scorn from without to borrow.
Old maxims these—yet stout and true—
 They speak in trumpet tone,
To do at once what is to do,
 And trust OURSELVES ALONE.

Too long our Irish hearts we schooled
 In patient hope to bide,
By dreams of English justice fooled
 And English tongues that lied.
That hour of weak delusion's past—
 The empty dream has flown:
Our hope and strength, we find at last,
 Is in OURSELVES ALONE.

Aye! bitter hate, or cold neglect,
    Or lukewarm love, at best,
Is all we've found, or can expect,
    We Aliens of the West.
No friend, beyond our own green shore,
    Can Erin truly own;
Yet stronger is her trust, therefore,
    In her brave sons ALONE.

Remember, when our lot was worse—
    Sunk, trampled to the dust—
'Twas long our weakness and our curse
    In stranger aid to trust.
And if, at length, we proudly trod
    On bigot laws o'erthrown,
Who won that struggle? Under God,
    Ourselves—OURSELVES ALONE.

Oh! let its memory be enshrined
    In Ireland's heart for ever!
It proves a banded people's mind
    Must win in just endeavor;
It shows how wicked to despair,
    How weak to idly groan—
If ills at *others'* hands ye bear,
    The cure is in YOUR OWN.

The foolish word " impossible"
    At once, for aye, disdain;
No power can bar a people's will,
    A people's right to gain.

Be bold, united, firmly set,
  Nor flinch in word or tone—
We'll be a glorious nation yet,
  REDEEMED—ERECT—ALONE!

SLIABH CUILINN.

THE LION AND THE SERPENT.

AN ARMS-BILL FABLE.

BY R. D. WILLIAMS.

IN days of old the Serpent came
  To the Lion's rocky hall,
And the forest king spread the sward with game,
  And they drank at the torrent's fall;
And the Serpent saw that the woods were fair,
And she longed to make her dwelling there.

But she saw that her host had a knack of his own
At tearing a sinew or cracking a bone,
  And had grinders unpleasantly strong;
So she said to herself: "I'll bamboozle the king
With my plausible speech, and all that sort of thing,
  That, since Eve, to my people belong."

"Those claws and those grinders must certainly be
Inconvenient to you as they're dreadful to me—
  Draw 'em out, like a love, I'm so 'frighted!
And, then, since I've long had an amorous eye on
Yourself and your property, dear Mr. Lion,
  We can be (spare my blushes) *united*."

So subtle the pow'r of her poisonous kisses,
So deadly to honor the falsehood she hisses,
   The Lion for once is an ass.
Before her, disarmed, the poor simpleton stands;
The union's proclaimed, but the hymen'al bands
   Are ponderous fetters of brass.

The Lion, self-conquered, is chained on the ground,
And the breath of his tyrant sheds poison around
   The fame and the life of her slave.
How long in his torture the stricken king lay
Historians omit, but 'tis known that one day
   The serpent began to look grave.

For, when passing, as usual, her thrall with a sneer,
She derisively hissed some new taunt in his ear,
   He shook all his chains with a roar;
And, observing more closely, she saw with much
   pain
That his tusks and his claws were appearing again,
   A fact she neglected before.

From that hour she grew *dang'rously civil*, indeed,
And declared he should be, ere long, totally freed
   From every dishonoring chain.
" The moment, my *dearest*, our friend, the Fox
   draws
Those nasty sharp things from your majesty's jaws,
   You must bound free as air o'er the plain."

But the captive sprang from his dungeon floor,
And he bowed the woods with a scornful roar,
   And his burning eyes flashed flame;
And as echo swelled the shout afar,
The stormy joy of freedom's war
   O'er the blast of the desert came.

And the Lion laughed, and his mirth was loud
As the stunning burst of a thunder-cloud,
   And he shook his wrathful mane;
And hollow sounds from his lashed sides come,
Like the sullen roll of a 'larum drum—
   He snapped like a reed the chain;
And the Serpent saw that her reign was o'er
And, hissing, she fled from the Lion's roar.

THE WEST'S ASLEEP.

BY THOMAS DAVIS.

Air—"*The Brink of the White Rocks.*"*

When all beside a vigil keep,
The West's asleep, the West's asleep—
Alas! and well may Erin weep,
When Connaught lies in slumber deep.

---

* This air slightly differs, in the end of the second line, from the version in Bunting's third volume, and agrees with that to which Mr. Horncastle sang "The Herring is King." There is a totally different and still finer air known in the county Tipperary by the name of "The Brink of the White Rocks."

There lake and plain smile fair and free,
'Mid rocks—their guardian chivalry ;
Sing, oh ! let man learn liberty
From crashing wind and lashing sea.

That chainless wave and lovely land
Freedom and nationhood demand—
Be sure, the great God never planned
For slumbering slaves a home so grand.
And, long, a brave and haughty race
Honored and sentinelled the place—
Sing, oh ! not even their sons' disgrace
Can quite destroy their glory's trace.

For often, in O'Connor's van,
To triumph dashed each Connacht clan,
And fleet as deer the Normans ran
Through Coirrsliabh Pass and Ard Rathain ;*
And later times saw deeds as brave ;
And glory guards Clanricard's grave—
Sing, oh ! they died their land to save,
At Aughrim's slopes and Shannon's wave.

And if, when all a vigil keep,
The West's asleep, the West's asleep,
Alas ! and well may Erin weep
That Connacht lies in slumber deep.
But, hark ! some voice like thunder spake :
" *The West's awake, the West's awake* "—
Sing, oh ! hurrah ! let England quake,
We'll watch till death for Erin's sake !

* Vulgarly written Coriews and Ardrahan.

THE IRISH REAPER'S HARVEST HYMN.

BY JOHN KEEGAN.

All hail! Holy Mary, our hope and our joy!
Smile down, blessed Queen! on the poor Irish boy
Who wanders away from his dear beloved home;
O Mary! be with me wherever I roam.
   Be with me, O Mary!
   Forsake me not, Mary!

From the home of my fathers in anguish I go,
To toil for the dark-livered, cold-hearted foe,
Who mocks me, and hates me, and calls me a slave,
An alien, a savage—all names but a knave.
   But, blessed be Mary!
   My sweet, holy Mary!
The *bodagh** he never dare call me a knave.

From my mother's mud sheeling an outcast I fly,
With a cloud on my heart and a tear in my eye;
Oh! I burn as I think that if *Some One* would say,
"Revenge on your tyrants!"—but, Mary! I pray,
   From my soul's depth, O Mary!
   And hear me, sweet Mary!
For union and peace to old Ireland I pray.

The land that I fly from is fertile and fair,
And more than I ask or I wish for is there,

---

* *Bodagh*, a clown, a churl.

But *I* must not taste the good things that I see—
"There's nothing but rags and green rushes for
    me."*
        O mild Virgin Mary!
        O sweet Mother Mary!
Who keeps my rough hand from red murder but
    thee?

But sure in the end our dear freedom we'll gain,
And wipe from the green flag each Sassanach stain,
And oh! Holy Mary, your blessing we crave!
Give hearts to the timid, and hands to the brave;
        And then, Mother Mary!
        Our own blessed Mary!
Light liberty's flame in the hut of the slave!

ADIEU TO INNISFAIL.
BY R. D. WILLIAMS.
Air—"*The Cruiskeen Lawn.*"

Adieu!—the snowy sail
Swells her bosom to the gale,
And our bark from Innisfail
        Bounds away.
While we gaze upon thy shore,
That we never shall see more,
And the blinding tears flow o'er,
        We pray.

---

* Taken literally from a conversation with a young peasant on his way to reap the harvest in England.

Ma vuirneen! be thou long
In peace the queen of song—
In battle proud and strong
    As the sea.
Be saints thine offspring still,
True heroes guard each hill,
And harps by ev'ry rill
    Sound free!

Though, round her Indian bowers,
The hand of nature showers
The brightest, blooming flowers
    Of our sphere;
Yet not the richest rose
In an *alien* clime that blows,
Like the briar at home that grows
    Is dear.

Though glowing breasts may be
In soft vales beyond the sea,
Yet ever, *gra ma chree*,
    Shall I wail
For the heart of love I leave,
In the dreary hours of eve,
On thy stormy shores to grieve,
    Innisfail!

But mem'ry o'er the deep
On her dewy wing shall sweep,
When in midnight hours I weep
    O'er thy wrongs;

And bring me, steeped in tears,
The dead flowers of other years,
And waft unto my ears
    Home's songs.

When I slumber in the gloom
Of a nameless, foreign tomb,
By a distant ocean's boom,
    Innisfail !
Around thy em'rald shore
May the clasping sea adore,
And each wave in thunder roar,
    " All hail !"

And when the final sigh
Shall bear my soul on high,
And on chainless wing I fly
    Through the blue,
Earth's latest thought shall be,
As I soar above the sea,
' Green Erin, dear, to thee
    Adieu !"

BOYHOOD'S YEARS.

BY THE REV. CHARLES MEEHAN.

AH ! why should I recal them—the gay, the joyous
  years,
Ere hope was crossed or pleasure dimmed by sorrow
  and by tears ?

Or why should mem'ry love to trace youth's glad
    and sunlit way,
When those who made its charms so sweet are
    gathered to decay?
The summer's sun shall come again to brighten
    hill and bower—
The teeming earth its fragrance bring beneath the
    balmy shower;   [our tears—
But all in vain will mem'ry strive—in vain we shed
They're gone away, and can't return—the friends
    of boyhood's years!

Ah! why, then, wake my sorrow, and bid me now
    count o'er   [to come no more—
The vanished friends so dearly prized—the days
The happy days of infancy, when no guile our
    bosoms knew,   [moment flew?
Nor recked we of the pleasures that with each
'Tis all in vain to weep for them—the past a dream
    appears;
And where are they—the loved, the young, the
    friends of boyhood's years?

Go seek them in the cold churchyard—they long
    have stolen to rest;
But do not weep, for their young cheeks by woe
    were ne'er oppressed.
Life's sun for them in splendor set—no cloud came
    o'er the ray
That lit them from this gloomy world upon their
    joyous way.

No tears about their graves be shed—but sweetest
    flow'rs be flung—   [perish young—
The fittest off'ring thou canst make to hearts that
To hearts this world has never torn with racking
    hopes and fears ;   [happy years!
For blessed are they who pass away in boyhood's

THE MEN OF TIPPERARY.

BY THOMAS DAVIS.

Let Britain boast her British hosts,
    About them all right little care we ;
Not British seas nor British coasts
    Can match the Man of Tipperary !

Tall is his form, his heart is warm,
    His spirit light as any fairy—
His wrath is fearful as the storm
    That sweeps the Hills of Tipperary.

Lead him to fight for native land,
    His is no courage cold and wary ;
The troops live not on earth would stand
    The headlong Charge of Tipperary !

Yet meet him in his cabin rude,
    Or dancing with his dark-haired Mary,
You'd swear they knew no other mood
    But mirth and love in Tipperary !

You're free to share his scanty meal—
   His plighted word he'll never vary;
In vain they tried with gold and steel
   To shake the Faith of Tipperary!

Soft is his *cailin's* sunny eye,
   Her mien is mild, her step is airy,
Her heart is fond, her soul is high—
   Oh! she's the Pride of Tipperary!

Let Britain, too, her banner brag,
   We'll lift the Green more proud and airy;
Be mine the lot to bear that flag,
   And head the Men of Tipperary.

Though Britain boasts her British hosts,
   About them all right little care we;
Give us, to guard our native coasts,
   The Matchless Men of Tipperary!

FATHER MATHEW.

ODE TO A PAINTER ABOUT TO COMMENCE A PICTURE ILLUSTRATING THE LABORS OF FATHER MATHEW.

Seize thy pencil, child of art!
   Fame and fortune brighten o'er thee!
Great thy hand, and great thy heart,
   If well thou dost the work before thee!

'Tis not thine to round the shield,
    Or point the sabre, black or gory;
'Tis not thine to spread the field,
    Where crime is crowned—where guilt is glory!

Child of art! to thee be given
    To paint, in colors all unclouded,
Breakings of a radiant heaven
    O'er an isle in darkness shrouded!
But, to paint them true and well,
    Every ray we see them shedding
In its very light must tell
    What a gloom *before* was spreading.

Canst thou picture dried-up tears—
    Eyes that wept no longer weeping—
Faithful woman's wrongs and fears,
    Lonely, nightly vigils keeping—
Listening every footfall nigh,
    Hoping him she loves returning?
Canst thou, then, depict her joy,
    That we may know *the change* from mourning?

Paint in colors strong, but mild,
    Our isle's redeemer and director.
Canst thou paint *the man* a *child*,
    Yet shadow forth the mighty VICTOR?
Let his path a rainbow span,
    Every *hue* and *color* blending,
Beaming "peace and love" to man,
    And alike o'er ALL extending!

Canst thou paint a land made free—
　From its sleep of bondage woken—
Yet, withal, that we may see
　What 'twas *before* the chain was broken?
Seize thy pencil, child of art!
　Fame and fortune brighten o'er thee!
Great thy hand, and great thy heart,
　If well thou dost the work before thee!

SONG OF THE PENAL DAYS.
A.D. 1720.
BY EDWARD WALSH.
Air—"*Mo Chraoivin Aovinn.*"

Ye dark-haired youths and elders hoary,
　List to the wand'ring harper's song.
My *clairseach* weeps my true love's story,
　In my true love's native tongue:
She's bound and bleeding 'neath the oppressor,
　Few her friends and fierce her foe,
And brave hearts cold who would redress her—
　Ma chreevin evin alga, O!

My love had riches once and beauty,
　Till want and sorrow paled her cheek;
And stalwart hearts for honor's duty—
　They're crouching now, like cravens sleek.
O Heaven! that e'er this day of rigor
　Saw sons of heroes abject, low—
And blood and tears thy face disfigure,
　Ma chreevin evin alga, O!

I see young virgins step the mountain
    As graceful as the bounding fawn,
With cheeks like heath-flow'r by the fountain,
    And breasts like downy *ceanavan*.
Shall bondsmen share those beauties ample?
    Shall their pure bosoms' current flow
To nurse new slaves for them that trample?
    Ma chreevin evin alga, O !

Around my *clairseach's* speaking measures
    Men, like their fathers tall, arise;
Their heart the same deep hatred treasures—
    I read it in their kindling eyes!
The same proud brow to frown at danger—
    The same long *coulin's* graceful flow—
The same dear tongue to curse the stranger—
    Ma chreevin evin alga, O !

I'd sing ye more, but age is stealing
    Along my pulse and tuneful fires;
Far bolder woke my chord, appealing,
    For craven *Sheamus*, to your sires.
Arouse to vengeance, men of brav'ry,
    For broken oaths—for altars low—
For bonds that bind in bitter slav'ry—
    Ma chreevin evin alga, O !

WAS IT A DREAM?

BY JOHN O'CONNELL.

It was an empty dream, perchance, yet seemed a
 vision high,
That in the midnight hour last night arose before
 mine eye—
Two figures—one in woe and chains, the other
 proud and free—
Were met in converse deep and grave beside the
 western sea.

" What, ne'er content, and restless still ?" the proud
 one sternly cried ;
" Forsooth of freedom prattling still, and parting
 from my side?
I hold thy chain, thou busy fool! mine ire thou
 mayest provoke,
And bring destruction on thine head, but never
 shake my yoke!"

Then up arose the mourning one, and raised her
 beauteous head,
And mild and calm, though sad in tone, " My sister," thus she said,   [thou hast been—
" For sister I would fain thee call, though tyrant
None feller or more pitiless hath hapless slave
 e'er seen.

" The rights, the freedom that I seek, the Lord of
    heaven gave—
That mighty Lord who never willed that earth
    should have a slave !—   [ask of thee
Those rights, that freedom thou didst take ; I only
To give *mine own* to me again, and friends we'll
    ever be."

The proud one laughed in haughty scorn, and
    waved a falchion bright   [the fight ;
O'er the enchained one's head aloft, and dared her to
The flushing cheek and kindling eye bespoke no
    terror there,
But, with a strong, convulsive gasp, she bowed to
    heaven in prayer !

Then raised her front serene again, and mildly spoke
    once more :   [passed o'er—
" Seven long and weary centuries of insult have
Of insult and of cruel wrong ! and from the earliest
    hour,   [of pow'r.
E'en to this day, a tyrant thou hast been in pride

" But when distress and enemies came threat'n-
    ingly around,   [been found !
Then soft in words, and falsely kind, thou ever hast
Distress again may come to thee, and foreign dan-
    gers press,   [thankfulness !"
And thou be forced to yield me all, and earn no

Again the proud one scornful laughed, and waved
    again her brand;   [fettered hand—
The other mutely raised to heaven her chained and
Then swift a storm passed o'er the scene, and when
    its gloom was gone,
The tyrant form was lowly laid—the captive had
    her own!

THE PATRIOT'S BRIDE.

BY CHARLES GAVAN DUFFY.

Oh! give me back that royal dream
    My fancy wrought,
When I have seen your sunny eyes
    Grow moist with thought,
And fondly hoped, dear love! your heart from mine
    Its spell had caught,
And laid me down to dream that dream, divine,
    But true, methought,
Of how my life's long task would be, to make yours
    blessed as it ought.

To learn to love sweet Nature more
    For your sweet sake,
To watch with you—dear friend! with you—
    Its wonders break;
The sparkling Spring in that bright face to see
    Its mirror make—

On Summer morns to hear the sweet birds sing
        By linn and lake ;
And know your voice, your magic voice, could still
    a grander music wake!

On some old, shell-strewn rock to sit
        In Autumn eves,
Where gray Killiney cools the torrid air
        Hot Autumn weaves ;
Or by that holy well in mountain lone,
        Where Faith believes
(Fain would I b'lieve) its secret, darling wish
        True love achieves :
Yet, oh! its saint was not more pure than she to
    whom my fond heart cleaves.

To see the dank, mid-winter night
        Pass like a noon,
Sultry with thought from minds that teemed
        And glowed like June;
Whereto would pass in sculped and pictured train
        Art's magic boon,
And Music thrill with many a haughty strain
        And dear old tune,
Till hearts grew sad to hear the destined hour to
    part had come so soon.

To wake the old, weird world that sleeps
        In Irish lore ;
The strains sweet, foreign Spenser sung
        By Mulla's shore ;

Dear Curran's airy thoughts, like purple birds
    That shine and soar;
Tone's fiery hopes, and all the deathless vows
    That Grattan swore;
The songs that once our own dear Davis sung—ah
    me! to sing no more.

To search with mother-love the gifts
    Our land can boast—
Soft Erna's isles, Neagh's wooded slopes,
    Clare's iron coast;
Kildare, whose legends gray our bosoms stir
    With fay and ghost;
Gray Mourne, green Antrim, purple Glenmalur,
    Lene's fairy host;
With raids to many a foreign land, to learn to love
    dear Ireland most.

And all those proud, old, victor fields
    We thrill to name,
Whose mem'ries are the stars that light
    Long nights of shame;
The cairn, the dun, the rath, the tower, the keep,
    That still proclaim,
In chronicles of clay and stone, how true, how deep
    Was Eiré's fame.
Oh! we shall see them all, with her, that dear, dear
    friend we two have loved the same.

Yet, ah! how truer, tend'rer still
    Methought did seem

That scene of tranquil joy, that happy home,
    By Dodder's stream ;
The morning smile, that grew a fixèd star
    With love-lit beam,
The ringing laugh, locked hands, and all the far
    And shining stream
Of daily love, that made our daily life diviner than
    a dream.

For still to me, dear friend ! dear love !
    Or both—dear wife !
Your image comes with serious thoughts,
    But tender, rife ;
No idle plaything, to caress or chide
    In sport or strife ;
But my best, chosen friend, companion, guide,
    To walk through life,
Linked hand in hand, two equal, loving friends,
    true husband and true wife.

THE LOST PATH.

BY THOMAS DAVIS.

Air—"*Gradh mo chroidhe.*"*

Sweet thoughts, bright dreams, my comfort be,
  All comfort else has flown ;
For every hope was false to me,
  And here I am, alone.

Vulgo, "*gra ma chrea*" (Anglice, my heart's love)

What thoughts were mine in early youth !
   Like some old Irish song,
Brimful of love, and life, and truth,
   My spirit gushed along.

I hoped to right my native isle,
   I hoped a soldier's fame,
I hoped to rest in woman's smile,
   And win a minstrel's name.
Oh ! little have I served my land,
   No laurels press my brow,
I have no woman's heart or hand,
   Nor minstrel honors now.

But fancy has a magic power ;
   It brings me wreath and crown,
And woman's love the self-same hour
   It smites oppression down.
Sweet thoughts, bright dreams, my comfort be,
   I have no joy beside ;
Oh ! throng around, and be to me
   Power, country, fame, and bride.

BIDE YOUR TIME.
BY M. J. BARRY.

BIDE YOUR TIME—the morn is breaking,
   Bright with freedom's blessed ray—
Millions, from their trance awaking,
   Soon shall stand in firm array.

Man shall fetter man no longer!
  Liberty shall march sublime:
Every moment makes you stronger—
  Firm, unshrinking, BIDE YOUR TIME.

BIDE YOUR TIME—one false step taken
  Perils all you yet have done;
Undismayed, erect, unshaken,
  Watch and wait, and all is won.
'Tis not by a rash endeavor
  Men or states to greatness climb:
Would you win your rights for ever,
  Calm and thoughtful, BIDE YOUR TIME.

BIDE YOUR TIME—your worst transgression
  Were to strike, and strike in vain.
He, whose arm would smite oppression,
  Must not need to smite again!
Danger makes the brave man steady—
  Rashness is the coward's crime;
Be for Freedom's battle ready
  When it comes—but, BIDE YOUR TIME.

THE PRICE OF FREEDOM.

BY D. F. M'CARTHY.

MAN of Ireland!—heir of sorrow!
  Wronged, insulted, scorned, oppressed—
Wilt thou never see that morrow
  When thy weary heart may rest?

Lift thine eyes, thou outraged creature!
  Nay, look up, for *man* thou art—
Man in form, in frame, and feature—
  Why not act man's godlike part?

Think, reflect, inquire, examine,
  Is't for this God gave you birth—
With the spectre look of famine
  Thus to creep along the earth?
Does this world contain no treasures
  Fit for thee, as man, to wear?—
Does this life abound in pleasures,
  And thou askest not to share?

Look! the nations are awaking—
  Every chain that bound them burst!
At the crystal fountains slaking
  With parched lips their fever thirst;
Ignorance, the demon, fleeing,
  Leaves unlocked the fount they sip—
Wilt thou not, thou wretched being,
  Stoop and cool thy burning lip?

History's lessons, if thou'lt read 'em,
  All proclaim this truth to thee:
Knowledge is the price of freedom—
  Know thyself, and thou art free!
Know, O man! thy proud vocation—
  Stand erect, with calm, clear brow—
Happy, happy were our nation
  If thou hadst that knowledge now!

Know thy wretched, sad condition—
    Know the ills that keep thee so;
Knowledge is the sole physician—
    Thou wert healed, if thou didst know!
Those who crush, and scorn, and slight thee—
    Those to whom you once would kneel—
Were the foremost then to right thee,
    If thou felt as thou shouldst feel.

Not as beggars lowly bending—
    Not in sighs, and groans, and tears—
But a voice of thunder sending
    Through thy tyrant brother's ears!
Tell him he is not thy master—
    Tell him of man's common lot;
Feel life has but one disaster—
    To be a slave, and know it not!

If thou knew what knowledge giveth—
    If thou knew how blest is he
Who in Freedom's presence liveth,
    Thou wouldst die, or else be free!
Round about he looks in gladness,
    Joys in heaven, and earth, and sea—
Scarcely heaves a sigh of sadness,
    Save in thoughts of such as thee!

INIS-EOGHAIN.

BY CHARLES GAVAN DUFFY.

(INIS-EOGHAIN (commonly written Innishowen, and pronounced Inni-shone) is a wild and picturesque district in the county Donegal, inhabited chiefly by the descendants of the Irish clans permitted to remain in Ulster after the plantation of James I. The native language and the old songs and legends of the country are as universal as the people. One of the most familiar of these legends is, that a troop of Hugh O'Neill's horse lies in magic sleep in a cave under the hill of Aileach, where the princes of the country were formerly installed. These bold troopers only wait to have the spell removed to rush to the aid of their country; and a man (says the legend) who wandered accidentally into the cave found them lying beside their horses, fully armed, and holding the bridles in their hands. One of them lifted his head, and asked, "Is the time come?" but receiving no answer—for the intruder was too much frightened to reply—dropped back into his lethargy. Some of the old folk consider the story an allegory, and interpret it as they desire.

God bless the gray mountains of dark Dun na n-
  gall!*
God bless royal Aileach! the pride of them all;
For she sits, evermore, like a queen on her throne,
And smiles on the valleys of green Inis-Eoghain.
  And fair are the valleys of green Inis-Eoghain,
  And hardy the fishers that call them their own—
  A race that nor traitor nor coward has known
  Enjoys the fair valleys of green Inis-Eoghain.

Oh! simple and bold are the bosoms they bear,
  Like the hills that with silence and nature they
    share;
For our God, who hath planted their home near
  his own,
Breath'd His Spirit abroad upon fair Inis-Eoghain.

* Donegal.

Then praise to our Father for wild Inis-Eoghain,
Where fiercely for ever the surges are thrown;
Nor weather nor fortune a tempest hath blown
Could shake the strong bosoms of brave Inis-
    Eoghain.

See the beautiful Cul-daim* carcering along,
A type of their manhood so stately and strong—
On the weary for ever its tide is bestown,
So they share with the stranger in fair Inis-Eoghain.
    God guard the kind homesteads of fair Inis-
        Eoghain,   [own;
    Which manhood and virtue have chosen for their
    Not long shall the nation in slavery groan
    That rears the tall peasants of fair Inis-Eoghain.

Like the oak of St. Bride, which nor devil nor Dane,
Nor Saxon nor Dutchman, could rend from her fane,
They have clung by the creed and the cause of their
        own,   Eoghain.
Through the midnight of danger, in true Inis-
    Then shout for the glories of old Inis-Eoghain,
    The stronghold that foeman has never o'er-
        thrown—
    The soul and the spirit, the blood and the bone,
    That guard the green valleys of true Inis-
        Eoghain.

* The Couldah, or Culdaff, is a chief river in the Innishowen mountains.

Nor purer of old was the tongue of the Gael
When the charging *aboo* made the foreigner quail,
Than it gladdens the stranger in welcome's soft tone
In the home-loving cabins of kind Inis-Eoghain.
    Oh! flourish, ye homesteads of kind Inis-Eoghain,
    Where seeds of a people's redemption are sown ;
    Right soon shall the fruit of that sowing have
        grown,
    To bless the kind homesteads of Green Inis-
        Eoghain.

When they tell us the tale of a spell-stricken band,
All entranced, with their bridles and broadswords
        in hand,
Who await but the word to give Erin her own,
They can read you that riddle in proud Inis-
        Eoghain !
    Hurrah for the spæmen* of proud Inis-Eoghain !
    Long live the wild seers of stout Inis-Eoghain ;
    May Mary, our mother, be deaf to their moan
    Who love not the promise of proud Inis-Eoghain!

PADDIES EVERMORE.

AIR—"*Paddies Evermore.*"

    The hour is past to fawn or crouch
        As suppliants for our right ;
    Let word and deed unshrinking vouch
        The banded millions' might :

---

* An Ulster and Scotch term signifying a person gifted with
" second sight"— a prophet.

Let them who scorned the fountain rill
    Now dread the torrent's roar,
And hear our echoed chorus still,
    We're Paddies evermore.

What, though they menace? suffering men
    Their threats and them despise;
Or promise justice once again?
    We know their words are lies:
We stand resolved those rights to claim
    They robbed us of before,
Our own dear nation and our name,
    As Paddies evermore.

Look round—the Frenchman governs France,
    The Spaniard rules in Spain,
The gallant Pole but waits his chance
    To break the Russian chain;
The strife for freedom here begun
    We never will give o'er,
Nor own a land on earth but one—
    We're Paddies evermore.

That strong and single love to crush
    The despot ever tried—
A fount it was whose living gush
    His hated arts defied.
'Tis fresh as when his foot accursed
    Was planted on our shore,
And now and still, as from the first,
    We're Paddies evermore.

What recked we though six hundred years
    Have o'er our thraldom rolled?
The soul that roused O'Connor's spears
    Still lives as true and bold.
The tide of foreign power to stem
    Our fathers bled of yore;
And we stand here to-day, like them,
    True Paddies evermore.

Where's our allegiance? With the land
    For which they nobly died;
Our duty? By our cause to stand,
    Whatever chance betide;
Our cherished hope? To heal the woes
    That rankle at her core;
Our scorn and hatred? To her foes,
    Like Paddies evermore.

The hour is past to fawn or crouch
    As suppliants for our right;
Let word and deed unshrinking vouch
    The banded millions' might;
Let them who scorned the fountain rill
    Now dread the torrent's roar,
And hear our echoed chorus still,
    We're Paddies evermore.

                    SLIABH CUILINN.

THE RIGHT ROAD.

BY THOMAS DAVIS.

Let the feeble-hearted pine,
Let the sickly spirit whine,
But to work and win be thine
    While you've life.
God smiles upon the bold—
So, when your flag's unrolled,
Bear it bravely till your cold
    In the strife.

If to rank or fame you soar,
Out your spirit frankly pour—
Men will serve you and adore,
    Like a king.
Woo your girl with honest pride,
'Till you've won her for your bride—
Then to her through time and tide
    Ever cling.

Never under wrongs despair,
Labor long and everywhere,
Link your countrymen, prepare,
    And strike home.
Thus have great men ever wrought,
Thus must greatness still be sought,
Thus labored, loved, and fought
    Greece and Rome.

A RALLY FOR IRELAND.

May, 1689.

BY THOMAS DAVIS.

Shout it out till it ring
   From Beinn-Mor to Cape Cleir,
For our country and king,
   And religion so dear,
     Rally, men, rally!
     Irishmen, rally!
Gather round the dear flag, that, wet with our tears,
And torn and bloody, lay hid for long years,
And now, once again, in its pride re-appears.
   See! from the castle our green banner waves,
   Bearing fit motto for uprising slaves—
     For "Now or never!
     Now and for ever!"
Bids you to battle for triumphs or graves—
Bids you to burst on the Sassanach knaves.
     Rally, then, rally!
     Irishmen, rally!
     Shout "Now or never!
     Now and for ever!"
   Heed not their fury, however it raves;
   Welcome their horsemen with pikes and with staves;

Close on their cannon, their bay'nets and
    glaives,
Down with their standard wherever it waves;
Fight to the last, and ye cannot be slaves!
Fight to the last, and ye cannot be slaves!

    Gallant Sheldon is here,
      And Hamilton, too,
    And Tirconaill so dear,
      And MacCarthy so true.
        And there are Frenchmen—
        Skilful and staunch men—
De Rosen, Pontee, Pusignan, and Boisseleau,
And gallant Lauzun is a-coming, you know,
With Bealdearg, the kinsman of great Owen Roe;
    From Sionainn to Bann, and from Life to Laoi,*
    The country is rising for liberty.
        Though your arms are rude,
        If your courage be good,
    As the traitor fled will the stranger flee,
    At another Drom-mhor from "the Irishry."
        Arm peasant and lord!
        Grasp musket and sword!
        Grasp pike, staff, and skian!
        Give your horses the rein!
March in the name of his majesty—
Ulster and Munster unitedly—
Townsman and peasant, like waves of the sea,—
Leinster and Connacht to victory—

* These rivers are vulgarly named the Shannon, Liffey, and Lea.

Shoulder to shoulder for liberty!
Shoulder to shoulder for liberty!

    Kirk, Schomberg, and Churchill
      Are coming—what then?
    We'll drive them and Dutch Will
      To England again.
      We can laugh at each threat,
      For our parliament's met—
De Courcy, O'Brien, M'Domhnaill, Le Poer,
O'Neill, and St. Lawrence, and others *go leor*,
The choice of the land from Athlone to the shore
    They'll break the last link of the Sassanach
      chain—
    They'll give us the lands of our fathers again!
      Then up ye! and fight
      For your king and your right,
    Or ever toil on, and never complain,
    Though they trample your roof-tree, and rifle
      your fane.
      Rally, then, rally!
      Irishmen, rally!
      Fight "Now or never!
      Now and for ever!"
Laws are in vain without swords to maintain;
So, muster as fast as the fall of the rain:
Serried and rough as a field of ripe grain,
Stand by your flag upon mountain and plain:
Charge till yourselves or your foemen are slain!
Fight till yourselves or your foemen are slain!

EIRE A RUIN.

AIR—"*Eibhlin a Ruin.*"*

Long thy fair cheek was pale,
      Eire a ruin—
Too well it spake thy tale,
      Eire a ruin—
Fondly nursed hopes betrayed,
Gallant sons lowly laid,
All anguish there portrayed,
      Eire a ruin.

Long my dear *clairseach's* string
      Eire a ruin,
Sang but as captives sing,
      Eire a ruin,
'Twas sorrow's broken sigh
Blent with mirth's reckless cry,
Saddest of minstrelsy!
      Eire a ruin.

Still was it thine to cope,
      Eire a ruin—
Still against hope to hope,
      Eire a ruin,
Ever through blackest woe
Fronting that tyrant foe,
Whom thou shalt yet lay low,
      Eire a ruin.

* In vulgar spelling, *Eileen aroon.*

Though he should sue thee now,
>   *Eire a ruin,*
Heed not his traitor vow,
>   *Eire a ruin;*
When didst thou e'er believe,
When his false words receive,
But sorely thou didst grieve,
>   *Eire a ruin?*

Millions of hearts are thine,
>   *Eire a ruin;*
Millions as one combine,
>   *Eire a ruin;*
Closer in peril knit,
Patient, though passion-lit—
For such is triumph writ,
>   *Eire a ruin.*

Then let thy *clairseach* pour,
>   *Eire a ruin,*
Wailings of grief no more,
>   *Eire a ruin;*
But strains like flash of steel,
Kindling that fire of zeal
Which melts their chains who feel,
>   *Eire a ruin.*

Sliabh Cuilinn.

TONE'S GRAVE.

BY THOMAS DAVIS.

In Bodenstown churchyard there is a green grave,
And wildly along it the winter winds rave;
Small shelter, I ween, are the ruined walls there
When the storm sweeps down on the plains of Kildare.

Once I lay on that sod—it lies over Wolfe Tone—
And thought how he perished in prison alone,
His friends unavenged, and his country unfreed—
"Oh! bitter," I said, "is the patriot's meed!

"For in him the heart of a woman combined
With a heroic life and a governing mind:
A martyr for Ireland—his grave has no stone,
His name seldom named, and his virtues unknown."

I was woke from my dream by the voices and tread
Of a band who came into the home of the dead;
They carried no corpse, and they carried no stone,
And they stopped when they came to the grave of Wolfe Tone.

There were students and peasants, the wise and the brave,
And an old man who knew him from cradle to grave;

And children who thought me hard-hearted—for they,
On that sanctified sod, were forbidden to play.

But the old man, who saw I was mourning there, said :
" We come, sir, to weep where young Wolfe Tone is laid ;
And we're going to raise him a monument, too—
A plain one, yet fit for the simple and true."

My heart overflowed, and I clasped his old hand,
And I blessed him, and blessed every one of his band :
" Sweet, sweet 'tis to find that such faith can remain
To the cause, and the man so long vanquished and slain !"

. . . .

In Bodenstown churchyard there is a green grave,
And freely around it let winter winds rave :
Far better they suit him—the ruin and gloom—
Till Ireland, a nation, can build him a tomb.

THE SHAN VAN VACHT.*
A.D. 1176.
BY MICHAEL DOHENY.

The sainted isle of old,
    Says the *Shan Van Vacht,*
The sainted isle of old,
    Says the *Shan Van Vacht,*
The parent and the mould
Of the beautiful and bold,
Has her blithesome heart waxed cold?
    Says the *Shan Van Vacht.*

The Saxon and the Dane,
    Says the *Shan Van Vacht,*
The Saxon and the Dane,
    Says the *Shan Van Vacht,*
The Saxon and the Dane
Our immortal hills profane;
Oh! confusion seize the twain,
    Says the *Shan Van Vacht.*

What are the chiefs to do?
    Says the *Shan Van Vacht,*
What are the chiefs to do?
    Says the *Shan Van Vacht.*
What should the chieftains do
But to treat the hireling crew
To a touch of Brian Boru?
    Says the *Shan Van Vacht.*

* Properly *An T-Sean Bhean Bhochd.*

They came across the wave,
  Says the *Shan Van Vacht*,
They came across the wave,
  Says the *Shan Van Vacht*,
They came across the wave
But to plunder and enslave,
And should find a robber's grave,
  Says the *Shan Van Vacht*.

Then be the trusty brand,
  Says the *Shan Van Vacht*,
Then be the trusty brand,
  Says the *Shan Van Vacht*,
Then be the trusty brand
Firmly clutched in every hand,
And we'll scourge them from the land,
  Says the *Shan Van Vacht*.

There's courage yet and truth,
  Says the *Shan Van Vacht*,
There's courage yet and truth,
  Says the *Shan Van Vacht*;
There's a God above us all,
And, whatever may befall,
No invader shall enthrall,
  Says the *Shan Van Vacht*.

THE GATHERING OF THE NATION.
BY J. D. FRAZER.

Those scalding tears—those scalding tears
  Too long have fallen in vain—
Up with the banners and the spears,
And let the gathered grief of years
  Show sterner stuff than rain.
The lightning, in that stormy hour
  When forth defiance rolls,
Shall flash to scathe the Saxon pow'r,
But melt the links our long, long show'r
  Had rusted round our souls.

To bear the wrongs we can redress,
  To make *a thing of time*—
The tyranny we can repress—
Eternal by our dastardness
  Were crime—or worse than crime!
And we, whose *best* and *worst* was shame,
  From first to last, alike,
May take, at length, a loftier aim,
And struggle, since it is the same
To *suffer*—or to *strike*.

What hatred of perverted might
  The cruel hand inspires
That robs the linnet's eye of sight,
To make it sing both day and night!
  Yet thus they robbed our sires,

By blotting out the ancient lore
    Where every loss was shown—
Up with the flag! we stand before
The Saxons of the days of yore
    In Saxons of our own.

Denial met our just demands,
    And hatred met our love;
Till now, by heaven! for grasp of hands
We'll give them clash of battle-brands,
    And gauntlet 'stead of glove.
And may the Saxon stamp his heel
    Upon the coward's front
Who sheathes his own unbroken steel
Until for mercy tyrants kneel,
    Who forced us to the brunt!

THE GERALDINES.

BY THOMAS DAVIS.

The Geraldines! the Geraldines!—'tis full a thousand years
Since, 'mid the Tuscan vineyards, bright flashed their battle-spears;
When Capet seized the crown of France, their iron shields were known,
And their sabre-dint struck terror on the banks of the Garonne;

Across the downs of Hastings they spurred hard by William's side,
And the gray sands of Palestine with Moslem blood they dyed;
But never then, nor thence till now, have falsehood or disgrace [his face.
Been seen to soil Fitzgerald's plume, or mantle in

The Geraldines! the Geraldines!— 'tis true, in Strongbow's van, [began;
By lawless force, as conquerors, their Irish reign
And, oh! through many a dark campaign they proved their prowess stern,
In Leinster's plains, and Munster's vales, on king, and chief, and kerne:
But noble was the cheer within the halls so rudely won,
And gen'rous was the steel-gloved hand that had such slaughter done!
How gay their laugh! how proud their mien! you'd ask no herald's sign— [Geraldine.
Among a thousand you had known the princely

These Geraldines! these Geraldines!—not long our air they breathed,
Not long they fed on venison, in Irish water seethed,
Not often had their children been by Irish mothers nursed,
When from their full and genial hearts an Irish feeling burst!

The English monarchs strove in vain, by law, and
    force, and bribe,
To win from Irish thoughts and ways this " more
    than Irish" tribe ;
For still they clung to fosterage, to *breitheamh*,
    cloak, and bard :   [discard" ?
What king dare say to Geraldine, " Your Irish wife

Ye Geraldines! ye Geraldines! how royally ye
    reigned   [arts disdained :
O'er Desmond broad and rich Kildare, and English
Your sword made knights, your banner waved,
    free was your bugle call
By Gleann's* green slopes, and Daingean's† tide,
    from Bearbha's‡ banks to Eochaill.§
What gorgeous shrines, what *breitheamh*‖ lore, what
    minstrel feasts there were
In and around Magh Nuadhaid's¶ keep, and palace-
    filled Adare!
But not for rite or feast ye stayed when friend or
    kin were pressed ;
And foemen fled when "*Crom abu*"** bespoke
    your lance in rest.

Ye Geraldines! ye Geraldines! since Silken Thomas
    flung
King Henry's sword on council board, the English
    thanes among,

* *Angl.* Glyn.   † *Angl.* Dingle.   ‡ *Angl.* Barrow.
§ *Angl.* Youghal.   ‖ *Angl.* Brehon.   ¶ *Angl.* Maynooth.
** Formerly the war cry of the Geraldines; and now their motto.

Ye never ceased to battle brave against the
    English sway,
Though axe and brand and treachery your
    proudest cut away.
Of Desmond's blood through woman's veins passed
    on th' exhausted tide ;
His title lives—a Sassanach churl usurps the lion's
    hide :
And though Kildare tower haughtily, there's ruin
    at the root,
Else why, since Edward fell to earth, had such a
    tree no fruit ?

True Geraldines! brave Geraldines! as torrents
    mould the earth,
You channelled deep old Ireland's heart by con-
    stancy and worth :
When Ginckle leaguered Limerick, the Irish sol-
    diers gazed
To see if in the setting sun dead Desmond's
    banner blazed !
And still it is the peasants' hope upon the Cuir-
    reach's* mere,
"They live who'll see ten thousand men with good
    Lord Edward here."
So let them dream till brighter days, when, not by
    Edward's shade,
But by some leader true as he, their lines shall be
    arrayed !

          * *Angl.* Curragh.

These Geraldines! these Geraldines! rain wears away the rock,
And time may wear away the tribe that stood the battle's shock,
But ever, sure, while one is left of all that honored race,
In front of Ireland's chivalry is that Fitzgerald's place ;
And though the last were dead and gone, how many a field and town,
From Thomas Court to Abbeyfeile, would cherish their renown !
And men will say of valor's rise, or ancient powers decline,
"'Twill never soar, it never shone, as did the Geraldine."

The Geraldines! the Geraldines! and are there any fears
Within the sons of conquerors for full a thousand years?
Can treason spring from out a soil bedewed with martyr's blood?
Or has that grown a purling brook which long rushed down a flood?
By Desmond swept with sword and fire, by clan and keep laid low,
By Silken Thomas and his kin, by sainted Edward! No!

The forms of centuries rise up, and in the Irish
    line
COMMAND THEIR SONS TO TAKE THE POST THAT FITS
    THE GERALDINE!*

HYMN OF FREEDOM.

BY M. J. BARRY.

GOD of peace! before thee,
    Peaceful, here we kneel,
Humbly to implore thee
    For a nation's weal.
Calm her sons' dissensions,
    Bid their discord cease,
End their mad contentions—
    Hear us, God of peace!

God of love! low bending,
    To thy throne we turn;
Let thy rays, descending,
    Through our island burn.
Let no strife divide us,
    But, from heaven above,
Look on us and guide us—
    Hear us, God of Love!

* The concluding stanza, now first published, was found among the Editor's papers.—E.D.

God of Battles! aid us;
   Let no despot's might
Trample or degrade us,
   Seeking this our right!
Arm us for the danger;
   Keep all craven fear
To our breasts a stranger—
   God of Battles! hear.

God of Right! preserve us
   Just—as we are strong;
Let no passion swerve us
   To one act of wrong;
Let no thought unholy
   Come our cause to blight;
Thus we pray thee, lowly—
   Hear us, God of Right!

God of Vengeance! smite us
   With thy shaft sublime,
If one bond unite us
   Forged in fraud or crime!
But if, humbly kneeling,
   We implore thine ear,
For our rights appealing—
   God of Nations! hear.

THE UNION.

How did they pass the Union?
  By perjury and fraud;
By slaves who sold their land for gold,
  As Judas sold his God;
By all the savage acts that yet
  Have followed England's track—
The pitchcap and the bayonet,
  The gibbet and the rack.
    And thus was passed the Union,
      By Pitt and Castlereagh;
    Could Satan send for such an end
      More worthy tools than they?

How thrive we by the Union?
  Look round our native land:
In ruined trade and wealth decayed
  See slavery's surest brand;
Our glory as a nation gone;
  Our substance drained away;
A wretched province trampled on,
  Is all we've left to-day.
    Then curse with me the Union,
      That juggle foul and base—
    The baneful root that bore such fruit
      Of ruin and disgrace.

And shall it last, this Union,
  To grind and waste us so?
O'er hill and lea, from sea to sea,
  All Ireland thunders, No!
Eight million necks are stiff to bow—
  We know our might as men;
We conquered once before, and now
  We'll conquer once again,
    And rend the cursed Union,
      And fling it to the wind—
    And Ireland's laws in Ireland's cause
      Alone our hearts shall bind!
              SLIABH CUILINN

THE PEASANT GIRLS.

THE Peasant Girl of merry France,
  Beneath her trellised vine,
Watches the signal for the dance—
  The broad, red sun's decline.
'Tis there—and forth she flies with glee
  To join the circling band,
Whilst mirthful sounds of minstrelsy
  Are heard throughout the land.

And fair Italia's Peasant Girl,
  The Arno's banks beside,
With myrtle flowers, that shine like pearl,
  Will braid at eventide

Her raven locks; and to the sky,
    With eyes of liquid light,
Look up, and bid her lyre outsigh:
    "Was ever land so bright?"

The Peasant Girl of England see,
    With lip of rosy dye,
Beneath her sheltering cottage tree,
    Smile on each passer-by.
She looks on fields of yellow grain,
    Inhales the bean-flower's scent,
And seems, amid the fertile plain,
    An image of content.

The Peasant Girl of Scotland goes
    Across her Highland hill,
With cheek that emulates the rose,
    And voice the skylark's thrill.
Her tartan plaid she folds around,
    A many-coloured vest—
Type of what varied joys have found
    A home in her kind breast.

The Peasant Girl of Ireland, she
    Has left her cabin home,
Bearing white wreaths—what can it be
    Invites her thus to roam?
Her eye has not the joyous ray
    Should to her years belong;
And, as she wends her languid way,
    She carols no sweet song.

Oh! soon upon the step and glance
    Grief does the work of age ;
And it has been her hapless chance
    To open that dark page.
The happy harvest home was o'er—
    The fierce tithe-gatherer came,
And her young lover, in his gore,
    Fell by a murderous aim !

Then, well may youth's bright glance be gone
    For ever from that eye,
And soon will sisters weep upon
    The grave that she kneels by ;
And well may prouder hearts than those,
    That there place garlands, say :
" Have Ireland's peasant girls such woes ?—
    When will they pass away ?"

THE BATTLE-EVE OF THE BRIGADE.

BY THOMAS DAVIS.

Air—"*Contented I am.*"

The mess-tent is full, and the glasses are set,
And the gallant Count Thomond is president yet;
The vet'ran arose like an uplifted lance,
Crying, " Comrades, a health to the monarch of
    France !"
With bumpers and cheers they have done as he bade,
For King Louis is loved by the Irish Brigade.

"A health to King James," and they bent as they quaffed;
"Here's to George the *Elector!*" and fiercely they laughed;
"Good luck to the girls we wooed long ago,
Where Sionainn,* and Bearbha,† and Abhain-dubh‡ flow;"
"God prosper Old Ireland!" you'd think them afraid,
So pale grew the chiefs of the Irish Brigade.

"But, surely, that light cannot come from our lamp—
And that noise—are they *all* getting drunk in the camp?"
"Hurrah! boys, the morning of battle is come,
And the *generale's* beating on many a drum."
So they rush from the revel to join the parade,
For the van is the right of the Irish Brigade.

They fought as they revelled, fast, fiery, and true,
And, though victors, they left on the field not a few;
And they who survived fought and drank as of yore,
But the land of their heart's hope they never saw more,
For in far, foreign fields, from Dunkirk to Belgrade,
Lie the soldiers and chiefs of the Irish Brigade.

* Shannon.   † Barrow.   ‡ Avondhu, or Black-water.

THE SONGS OF THE NATION.

BY EDWARD WALSH.

Ye songs that resound in the homes of our island—
That wake the wild echoes by valley and highland—
That kindle the cold with their forefather's story—
That point to the ardent the pathway of glory!—
    Ye send to the banished,
      O'er ocean's far wave,
    The hope that had vanished,
      The vow of the brave ;
And teach each proud despot of loftiest station
To pale at your spell-word, sweet Songs of The Nation!

Sweet songs! ye reveal, through the vista of ages,
Our monarchs and heroes, our minstrels and sages,
The splendor of Eamhain,* the glories of Teamhair,†
When Erin was free from the Saxon defamer—
    The green banner flying,
      The rush of the Gael,
    The Sassanach's dying,
      His matron's wild wail—
These glories forgotten, with magic creation,
Burst bright at your spell-word, sweet Songs of The Nation!

---

* The palace of the Ulster Kings, near Armagh, Latinised Emania.
† Tara.

The minstrels who waken these wild notes of
    freedom
Have hands for green Erin—if Erin should need
    'em ;
And hearts for the wronged one wherever he ranges,
From Zebla to China—from Sionainn* to Ganges ;
    And hate for his foeman,
        All hatred above ;
    And love for dear woman,
        The tenderest love ;
But chiefest the fair ones whose eyes' animation
Is the spell that inspires the sweet Songs of THE
    NATION !

THE DAY-DREAMER.

BY CHARLES GAVAN DUFFY.

WHAT joy was mine in the gallant time
    When I was an outlaw bold !
Girt with my clan in the glades of Truagh,
    Or shut in my castle-hold,
In solemn feis,† with the brehons gray,
    And the stalwart chiefs of old.

How many a trancèd hour I sat
    At the feet of the Soldier-Saint ;‡

---

* Shannon.   † Feis, the public council of the ancient Irish.
‡ St. Lorcan O'Tuthill.

Or drank high hopes from our dauntless Hugh
    That cordial the hearts of the faint;
Or wove bold plots with untiring Tone,
    To blot out the isle's attaint.

What deeds we vowed to the dear old land!
    What solemn words we spoke!
How never we'd cease or sleep in peace
    Till we shattered the stranger's yoke—
And not with a storm of windy words,
    But many a soldier stroke.

We'd knotted whips for the Saxon churls,
    And steel for the Norman peers,
And a gallows high for the pampered priests
    Who were drunk with the peasants' tears;
And the towers grim where the robbers laired,
    We dashed them about their ears!

We lifted the buried harp anew,
    With its guardian spear and skeane,*
And forth we sent to the listening land
    Full many a mystic strain,
Which scattered the slavish fear away
    That hung on its breast like a chain.

The torrent's voice in the slumb'ring night
    Is tame to the words we spake—

---

* Skeane, properly *Skian* the dagger of the Irish.

The tempest words in whose fiery breath
  The thrones and dominions shake;
Till, lo! from their sleep the people rose,
  And their chains like a reed they brake.

It stirs me still, that solemn sight,
  Of the proud old land made free,
Our flag afloat from her castles tall
  And the ships on the circling sea,
And the joyful voice, like a roll of drums,
  Of the nation's jubilee!

A BALLAD OF FREEDOM.

BY THOMAS DAVIS.

The Frenchman sailed in Freedom's name to smite the Algerine,
The strife was short, the crescent sunk, and then his guile was seen,
For, nestling in the pirate's hold—a fiercer pirate far—
He bade the tribes yield up their flocks, the towns their gates unbar.
Right on he pressed with freemen's hands to subjugate the free,
The Berber in old Atlas glens, the Moor in Titteri;
And wider had his *razzias* spread, his cruel conquests broader,

But God sent down, to face his frown, the gallant Abdel-Kader—
The faithful Abdel-Kader! unconquered Abdel-Kader!
   Like falling rock,
   Or fierce siroc—.
  No savage or marauder—
   Son of a slave!
   First of the brave!
  Hurrah for Abdel-Kader!*

The Englishman, for long, long years, had ravaged Ganges' side—
A dealer first, intriguer next, he conquered far and wide,
Till, hurried on by avarice and thirst of endless rule,
His sepoys pierced to Candahar, his flag waved in Cabul;
But still within the conquered land was one unconquered man,
The fierce Pushtani† lion, the fiery Akhbar Khan—
He slew the sepoys on the snow, till Scindh's‡ full flood they swam it

---

 * This name is pronounced Cawder. The French say that their great foe was a slave's son. Be it so—he has a hero's and freeman's heart. "Hurrah for Abdel-Kader!"

 † This is the name by which the Affghans call themselves. Affghan is a Persian name (see Elphinstone's delightful book on Cabul). Note, too, that in most of their words *a* sounds *aw*, *u* sounds *oo*, and *i* sounds *ee*.

 ‡ The real name of the Indus, which is a Latinised word.

Right rapidly, content to flee the son of Dost
    Mohammed,
The son of Dost Mohammed, the brave old Dost
    Mohammed!
        Oh! long may they
        Their mountains sway,
    Akhbar and Dost Mohammed!
        Long live the Dost,
        Who Britain crost—
    Hurrah for Dost Mohammed!

The Russian, lord of million serfs and nobles serflier
    still,   [will;
Indignant saw Circassia's sons bear up against his
With fiery ships he lines their coast, his armies
    cross their streams,
He builds a hundred fortresses—his conquest done,
    he deems.
But steady rifles—rushing steeds—a crowd of
    nameless chiefs!   [reefs.
The plough is o'er his arsenals!—his fleet is on the
The maidens of Kabyntica are clad in Moscow
    dresses—
His slavish herd, how dared they beard the moun-
    tain-bred Cherkesses!
The lightning Cherkesses! the thundering Cher-
    kesses!
        May Elburz top
        In Azof drop,

   Ere Cossacks beat Cherkesses !
    The fountain-head
    Whence Europe spread—
   Hurrah for the tall Cherkesses !*

But Russia preys on Poland's fields, where Sobieski
  reigned ;
And Austria on Italy—the Roman eagle chained—
Bohemia, Servia, Hungary, within her clutches gasp ;
And Ireland struggles gallantly in England's loosen-
  ing grasp.   [on alone,
Oh ! would all these their strength unite, or battle
Like Moor, Pushtani, and Cherkess, they soon
  would have their own.
Hurrah ! hurrah ! it can't be far, when from the
  Scindh to Sionainn†
Shall gleam a line of freemen's flags begirt with
  freemen's cannon !
The coming day of Freedom—the flashing flags of
  Freedom
     The victor glaive—
     The mottoes brave,
   May we be there to read them !
     That glorious noon,
     God send it soon—
   Hurrah ! for human freedom !

---

* Cherkesses or Abydes is the right name of the so-called Circassians Kabyntica is a town in the heart of the Caucasus, of which Mount Elburz is the summit. Blumenbach and other physiologists assert that the finer European races descend from a Circassian stock.

† Shannon.

"CEASE TO DO EVIL—LEARN TO DO WELL."*

BY D. F. M'CARTHY.

O THOU whom sacred duty hither calls,
   Some glorious hours in freedom's cause to dwell,
Read the mute lesson on thy prison walls—
   " Cease to do evil—learn to do well!"

If haply thou art one of genius vast,
   Of generous heart, of mind sublime and grand,
Who all the spring-time of thy life hast passed
   Battling with tyrants for thy native land—
If thou hast spent thy summer, as thy prime,
   The serpent brood of bigotry to quell,
Repent, repent thee of thy hideous crime—
   " Cease to do evil—learn to do well!"

If thy great heart beat warmly in the cause
   Of outraged man, whate'er his race might be—
If thou hast preached the Christian's equal laws,
   And stayed the lash beyond the Indian sea—
If at thy call a nation rose sublime—
   If at thy voice seven million fetters fell,
Repent, repent thee of thy hideous crime—
   " Cease to do evil—learn to do well!"

* Inscription on O'Connell's prison.

If thou hast seen thy country's quick decay,
    And, like a prophet, raised thy saving hand,
And pointed out the only certain way
    To stop the plague that ravaged o'er the land—
If thou hast summoned from an alien clime
    Her banished senate here at home to dwell,
Repent, repent thee of thy hideous crime—
    " Cease to do evil—learn to do well !"

Or if, perchance, a younger man thou art,
    Whose ardent soul in throbbings doth aspire,
Come weal, come woe, to play the patriot's part
    In the bright footsteps of thy glorious sire !
If all the pleasures of life's youthful time
    Thou hast abandoned for the martyr's cell,
Do thou repent thee of thy hideous crime—
    " Cease to do evil—learn to do well !"

Or art thou one whom early science led
    To walk with Newton through the immense of heaven,
Who soared with Milton, and with Mina bled,
    And all thou hadst in Freedom's cause hath given ?
Oh ! fond enthusiast—in the after time
    Our children's children of your worth shall tell !
England proclaims thy honesty a crime—
    " Cease to do evil—learn to do well !"

Or art thou one whose strong and fearless pen
  Roused the young isle, and bade it dry its tears,
And gathered round thee ardent, gifted men,
  The hope of Ireland in the coming years—
Who dares in prose and heart-awakening rhyme
  Bright hopes to breathe, and bitter truths to tell ?
Oh! dangerous criminal, repent thy crime—
  "Cease to do evil—learn to do well!"

"Cease to do evil"—aye! ye madmen, cease!
  Cease to love Ireland, cease to serve her well,
Make with her foes a foul and fatal peace,
  And quick will ope your darkest, dreariest cell.
"Learn to do well"—aye! learn to betray—
  Learn to revile the land in which you dwell;
England will bless you on your altered way—
  "Cease to do evil—learn to do well!"

  Third week of O'Connell's imprisonment.

THE SWORD.

BY M. J. BARRY.

What rights the brave?
    The sword!
What frees the slave?
    The sword!

What cleaves in twain
The despot's chain,
And makes his gyves and dungeons vain?
The sword!

CHORUS.

Then cease thy proud task never
While rests a link to sever!
Guard of the free,
We'll cherish thee,
And keep thee bright for ever!

What checks the knave?
The sword!
What smites to save?
The sword!
What wreaks the wrong
Unpunished long,
At last, upon the guilty strong?
The sword!

CHORUS.

Then cease thy proud task never, &c.

What shelters right?
The sword!
What makes it might?
The sword!

What strikes the crown
Of tyrants down,
And answers with its flash their frown ?
The sword !

CHORUS.

Then cease thy proud task never, &c.

Still be thou true,
Good sword !
We'll die or do,
Good sword !
Leap forth to light
If tyrants smite,
And trust our arms to wield thee right,
Good sword !

CHORUS.

Yes ! cease thy proud task never
While rests a link to sever !
Guard of the free,
We'll cherish thee,
And keep thee bright for ever !

A DREAM OF THE FUTURE.

BY D. F. M'CARTHY.

I DREAMT a dream, a dazzling dream, of a green isle far away,
Where the glowing west to the ocean's breast calleth the dying day;
And that island green was as fair a scene as ever man's eye did see,
With its chieftains bold, and its temples old, and its homes and its altars free!
No foreign foe did that green isle know—no stranger band it bore,
Save the merchant train from sunny Spain and from Afric's golden shore!
And the young man's heart would fondly start, and the old man's eye would smile,
As their thoughts would roam o'er the ocean foam to that lone and "holy isle!"

Years passed by, and the orient sky blazed with a new-born light,
And Bethlehem's star shone bright afar o'er the lost world's darksome night;
And the diamond shrines from plundered mines, and the golden fanes of Jove,
Melted away in the blaze of day at the simple spell-word, "love!"

The light serene o'er that island green played with
    its saving beams,
And the fires of Baal waxed dim and pale like the
    stars in the morning streams !
And 'twas joy to hear, in the bright air clear, from
    out each sunny glade,
The tinkling bell, from the quiet cell or the
    cloister's tranquil shade !

A cloud of night o'er that dream so bright soon
    with its dark wing came,
And the happy scene of that island green was lost
    in blood and shame ;
For its kings unjust betrayed their trust, and its
    queens, though fair, were frail,
And a robber band from a stranger land with
    their war-whoops filled the gale ;
A fatal spell on that green isle fell—a shadow of
    death and gloom
Passed withering o'er, from shore to shore, like the
    breath of the foul simoom ;
And each green hill's side was crimson dyed, and
    each stream rolled red and wild,
With the mingled blood of the brave and good—
    of mother, and maid, and child !

Dark was my dream, though many a gleam of hope
    through that black night broke,
Like a star's bright form through a whistling storm,
    or the moon through a midnight oak '

And many a time, with its wings sublime, and its
    robes of saffron light,
Would the morning rise on the eastern skies, but
    to vanish again in night!
For, in abject prayer, the people there still raised
    their fettered hands,
When the sense of right and the power to smite
    are the spirit that commands;
For those who would sneer at the mourner's tear,
    and heed not the suppliant's sigh,
Would bow in awe to that first great law—a
    banded nation's cry!

At length arose o'er that isle of woes a dawn with
    a steadier smile,
And in happy hour a voice of pow'r awoke the
    slumbering isle!
And the people all obeyed the call of their chief's
    unsceptred hand,
Vowing to raise as in ancient days the name of
    their own dear land!
My dream grew bright as the sun-beam's light, as
    I watched that isle's career
Through the varied scene and the joys serene of
    many a future year—
And, oh! what thrill did my bosom fill, as I gazed
    on a pillared pile,
Where a senate once more in power watched o'er
    the rights of that lone green isle!

THE EXTERMINATOR'S SONG.

BY JOHN CORNELIUS O'CALLAGHAN.

Air—"'*Tis I am the Gipsy King.*"

'Tis I am the poor man's scourge,
 And where is the scourge like me?
My land from all Papists I purge,
 Who think that their votes should be free,
 Who think that their votes should be free.
For huts only fitted for brutes
 My agent the last penny wrings;
And my serfs live on water and roots,
 While I feast on the best of good things!
  For I am the poor man's scourge!
  For I am the poor man's scourge!

(Chorus of the Editors of the Nation)
 Yes, *you* are the poor man's scourge!
 But of *such* the whole island we'll purge!

A despot, and a strong one, am I,
 Since a Drummond no longer is here
To my "*duties*" to point ev'ry eye,
 Though of "*rights*" I wish only to hear—
 Though of "*rights*" I wish only to hear!
If conspiracies I apprehend,
 To throw off my rack-renting rule,

For a "*Special Commission*" I send
   To my friends of the old Tory school,
     For I am the poor man's scourge!
     For I am the poor man's scourge!

us of the Editors of the Nation)
Yes, *you* are the poor man's scourge!
But of *such* the whole island we'll purge!

I prove to the world I'm a man,
   In a way very pleasant to show;
I corrupt all the tenants I can,
   And of children I have a long row—
   And of children I have a long row!
My cottiers must all cringe to me,
   Nor grudge me the prettiest lass;
Or they know very well that they'll see
   Their hovels as flat as the grass!
     For I am the poor man's scourge!
     For I am the poor man's scourge!

(Chorus of the Editors of the Nation)
Yes, *you* are the poor man's scourge!
But of *such* the whole island we'll purge!

If a Connor my right should deny
   To "do what I like with **my** own,"
For the rascal I've soon a reply,
   Into gaol for "*sedition*" he's thrown—
   Into gaol for "*sedition*" he's thrown!

The tariff is bringing rents down,
   Yet more cash from the farmer I'll squeeze;
And, for fear of being shot, come to town
   To drink, game, and intrigue at my ease!
     For I am the poor man's scourge!
     For I am the poor man's scourge!

(Chorus of the Editors of the Nation)
   Yes, *you* are the poor man's scourge!
   But of *such* the whole island we'll purge!

ANNIE, DEAR.

BY THOMAS DAVIS.

OUR mountain brooks were rushing,
            Annie, dear,
The Autumn eve was flushing,
            Annie, dear;
But brighter was your blushing,
When first, your murmurs hushing,
I told my love outgushing,
            Annie, dear.

Ah! but our hopes were splendid,
            Annie, dear,
How sadly they have ended,
            Annie, dear;

The ring betwixt us broken,
When our vows of love were spoken,
Of your poor heart was a token,
   Annie, dear.

The primrose flow'rs were shining,
   Annie, dear,
When, on my breast reclining,
   Annie, dear,
Began our *Mi-na-Meala*,
And many a month did follow
Of joy—but life is hollow,
   Annie, dear.

For once, when home returning,
   Annie, dear,
I found our cottage burning,
   Annie, dear;
Around it were the yeomen,
Of every ill an omen,
The country's bitter foemen,
   Annie, dear.

But why arose a morrow,
   Annie, dear,
Upon that night of sorrow,
   Annie, dear?
Far better by thee lying,
Their bayonets defying,
Than live an exile sighing
   Annie, dear.

A NEW YEAR'S SONG.

My countrymen, awake! arise!
  Our work begins anew:
Your mingled voices rend the skies,
  Your hearts are firm and true;
You've bravely marched and nobly met
  Our little green isle through,
But oh! my friends, there's something yet
  For Irishmen to do!

As long as Erin hears the clink
  Of base, ignoble chains—
As long as one detested link
  Of foreign rule remains—
As long as of our rightful debt
  One smallest fraction's due,
So long, my friends, there's something yet
  For Irishmen to do!

Too long we've borne the servile yoke,
  Too long the slavish chain,
Too long in feeble accents spoke,
  And ever spoke in vain.
Our wealth has filled the spoiler's net,
  And gorged the Saxon crew;
But, oh! my friends, we'll teach them yet
  What Irishmen can do!

The olive branch is in our hands,
　　The white flag floats above ;
Peace—peace pervades our myriad bands,
　　And proud, forgiving love ;
But, oh ! let not our foes forget
　　We're *men*, as Christians, too,
Prepared to do for Ireland yet
　　What Irishmen should do !

There's not a man of all our land
　　Our country now can spare,
The strong man with his sinewy hand,
　　The weak man with his pray'r !
No whining tone of mere regret,
　　Young Irish bards, for you ;
But let your songs teach Ireland yet
　　What Irishmen should do !

And wheresoe'er that duty lead,
　　There, there your post should be ;
The coward slave is never freed—
　　The brave alone are free !
O Freedom ! firmly fixed are set
　　Our longing eyes on you ;
And though we die for Ireland yet,
　　So Irishmen should do !

OH! FOR A STEED.

BY THOMAS DAVIS.

Oh! for a steed, a rushing steed, and a blazing scimitar,
To hunt from beauteous Italy the Austrian's red hussar;
    To mock their boasts,
    And strew their hosts,
And scatter their flags afar.

Oh! for a steed, a rushing steed, and dear Poland gathered around,
To smite her circle of savage foes, and smash them upon the ground;
    Nor hold my hand
    While on the land
A foreigner foe was found.

Oh! for a steed, a rushing steed, and a rifle that never failed,
And a tribe of terrible prairie men, by desperate valor mailed,
    Till "stripes and stars"
    And Russian czars
Before the Red Indian quailed.

Oh! for a steed, a rushing steed, on the plains of
    Hindostan,
And a hundred thousand cavaliers to charge like a
    single man,
        Till our shirts were red,
        And the English fled
      Like a cowardly caravan.

Oh! for a steed, a rushing steed, with the Greeks
    at Marathon,
Or a place in the Switzer phalanx, when the Morat
    men swept on
        Like a pine-clad hill
        By an earthquake's will
      Hurled the valleys upon.

Oh! for a steed, a rushing steed, when Brian smote
    down the Dane,
Or a place beside great Aodh O'Neill, when Bage-
    nal the bold was slain,
        Or a waving crest
        And a lance in rest
      With Bruce upon Bannoch plain.

Oh! for a steed, a rushing steed, on the Currach of
    Cildar,
And Irish squadrons skilled to do as they are ready
    to dare,
        A hundred yards,
        And England's guards
      Drawn up to engage me there.

Oh! for a steed, a rushing steed, and any good
    cause at all,
Or else, if you will, a field on foot, or guarding a
    leaguered wall,
        For Freedom's right
        In flushing fight
      To conquer, if then to fall.

THE VOICE AND PEN.

BY D. F. M'CARTHY.

OH! the orator's voice is a mighty power
    As it echoes from shore to shore;
And the fearless pen has more sway o'er men
    Than the murderous cannon's roar.
What burst the chain far o'er the main,
    And brightens the captive's den?
'Tis the fearless voice and the pen of power—
    Hurrah! for the Voice and Pen!
              Hurrah!
    Hurrah! for the Voice and Pen!

The tyrant knaves who deny our rights,
    And the cowards who blanch with fear,
Exclaim with glee, "No arms have ye—
    Nor cannon, nor sword, nor spear!

Your hills are ours; with our forts and tow'rs
    We are masters of mount and glen."
Tyrants, beware! for the arms we bear
    Are the Voice and the fearless Pen!
                      Hurrah!
    Hurrah! for the Voice and Pen!

Though your horsemen stand with their bridles in hand,
    And your sentinels walk around—
Though your matches flare in the midnight air
    And your brazen trumpets sound;
Oh! the orator's tongue shall be heard among
    These listening warrior men,
And they'll quickly say, "Why should we slay
    Our friends of the Voice and Pen?"
                      Hurrah!
    Hurrah! for the Voice and Pen!

When the Lord created the earth and sea,
    The stars and the glorious sun,
The Godhead *spoke*, and the universe woke,
    And the mighty work was done!
Let a word be flung from the orator's tongue,
    Or a drop from the fearless pen,
And the chains accursed asunder burst
    That fettered the minds of men
                      Hurrah!
    Hurrah! for the Voice and Pen!

Oh! these are the swords with which we fight,
   The arms in which we trust,
Which no tyrant hand will dare to brand,
   Which time cannot dim or rust!
When these we bore we triumphed before,
   With these we'll triumph again;
And the world will say, " No power can stay
   " The Voice and the fearless Pen!"
                        Hurrah!
   Hurrah! for the Voice and Pen!

UP FOR THE GREEN.

A SONG OF THE UNITED IRISHMEN.

A.D. 1796.

Air—*"The Wearing of the Green."*

'Tis the green—oh! the green is the color of the true,
And we'll back it 'gainst the orange, and we'll raise it o'er the blue!
And the color of our fatherland alone should here be seen—
And the color of the martyred dead—our own immortal green.
   Then up for the green, boys, and up for the green!
   Oh! 'tis down to the dust, and a shame to be seen;

But we've hands, oh! we've hands, boys, full
    strong enough, I ween,
To rescue and to raise again our own immortal
    green!

They may say they have power 'tis vain to oppose—
'Tis better to obey and live, than surely die as foes;
But we scorn all their threats, boys, whatever
    they may mean;
For we trust in God above us, and we dearly love
    the green.
    So we'll up for the green, and we'll up for the
        green—
    Oh! to *die* is far better than be cursed as we have
        been;
    And we've hearts—oh! we've hearts, boys, full
        true enough, I ween,
    To rescue and to raise again our own immor-
        tal green.

They may swear, as they often did, our wretched-
    ness to cure,
But we'll never trust John Bull again, nor let his
    lies allure;
No, we won't, no, we won't, Bull, for now nor ever
    more!
For we've hopes on the ocean, and we've trust on
    the shore.

    Then up for the green, boys, then up for the
        green !
    Shout it back to the Sassanach, " We'll *never* sell
        the green !"
    For our Tone is coming back, and with men
        enough, I ween,
    To rescue and avenge us and our own immortal
        green.

Oh ! remember the days when their reign we did
    disturb,
At *Luimneach** and *Durlas*†, Blackwater and
    Beinnbhorb,‡
And ask this proud Saxon if our blows he did en-
    joy
When we met him on the battle-field of France—at
    Fontenoy.
    Then we'll up for the green, boys, and up for
        the green !
    Oh ! 'tis *still* in the dust, and a shame to be
        seen ;
    But we've hearts and we've hands, boys, full
        strong enough, I ween,
    To rescue and to raise again our own unsul-
        lied green !
FERMOY.

* Limerick.   † Misspel- Thurles.   ‡ Benburb.

MY LAND.

BY THOMAS DAVIS.

She is a rich and rare land ;
Oh ! she's a fresh and fair land;
She is a dear and rare land—
   This native land of mine.

No men than hers are braver—
Her women's hearts ne'er waver ;
I'd freely die to save her,
   And think my lot divine.

She's not a dull or cold land ;
No ! she's a warm and bold land ;
Oh ! she's a true and old land—
   This native land of mine.

Could beauty ever guard her,
And virtue still reward her,
No foe would cross her border—
   No friend within it pine !

Oh ! she's a fresh and fair land,
Oh ! she's a true and rare land !
Yes, she's a rare and fair land—
   This native land of mine.

THE BOATMAN OF KINSALE.

BY THOMAS DAVIS.

Air—"*The Cota Caol.*"

His kiss is sweet, his word is kind,
   His love is rich to me;
I could not in a palace find
   A truer heart than he.
The eagle shelters not his nest
   From hurricane and hail
More bravely than he guards my breast—
   The Boatman of Kinsale.

The wind that round the Fastnet sweeps
   Is not a whit more pure;
The goat that down Cnoc Sheehy leaps
   Has not a foot more sure;
No firmer hand nor freer eye
   E'er faced an Autumn gale;
De Courcy's heart is not so high—
   The Boatman of Kinsale.

The brawling squires may heed him not,
   The dainty stranger sneer—
But who will dare to hurt our cot
   When Myles O'Hea is here?
The scarlet soldiers pass along—
   They'd like, but fear, to rail;
His blood is hot, his blow is strong—
   The Boatman of Kinsale.

His hooker's in the Scilly van
   When seines are in the foam ;
But money never made the man,
   Nor wealth a happy home.
So, blest with love and liberty,
   While he can trim a sail,
He'll trust in God, and cling to me—
   The Boatman of Kinsale.

LAMENT FOR THE MILESIANS.

BY THOMAS DAVIS.

Oh! proud were the chieftains of proud Innis-Fail,
   A's truagh gan oidhir 'n-a bh-farradh !*
The stars of our sky and the salt of our soil,
   A's truagh gan oidhir 'n-a bh-farradh :
Their hearts were as soft as a child in the lap—
Yet they were "the men in the gap;"
And now that the cold clay their limbs doth enwrap,
   A's truagh gan oidhir 'n-a bh-farradh !

---

* *A's truagh gan oidhir 'n a bh-farradh.* "That is pity, without heir in their company," *i.e.*, what a pity that there is no heir of their company. See the poem of Giolla Iosa Mor Mac Firbisigh, *The Genealogies, Tribes, and Customs of the Uí Fiachrach, or O'Dubhda's Country,* printed for the Irish Arch. Soc., p. 230, line 2, and note d. Also O'Reilly's *Dict*, voce *farradh*.

'Gainst England long battling, at length they went
    down,
    A's truagh gan oidhir 'n-a bh-farradh!
But they've left their deep tracks on the road of
    renown,
    A's truagh gan oidhir 'n-a bh-farradh !
We are heirs of their fame, if we're not of their race,
And deadly and deep our disgrace,
If we live o'er their sepulchres abject and base,
    A's truagh gan oidhir 'n-a bh-farradh !

Oh! sweet were the minstrels of kind Innis-Fail!
    A's truagh gan oidhir 'n-a bh-farradh !
Whose music nor ages nor sorrow can spoil,
    A's truagh gan oidhir 'n-a bh-farradh !
But their sad, stifled tones are like streams flowing
    hid,
Their caoine and their pibroch were chid,
And their language, "that melts into music,"
    forbid,
    A's truagh gan oidhir 'n-a bh-farradh !

How fair were the maidens of fair Innis-Fail,
    A's truagh gan oidhir 'n-a bh-farradh !
As fresh and as free as the sea-breeze from soil,
    A's truagh gan oidhir 'n-a bh-farradh !
Oh ! are not our maidens as fair and as pure?
Can our music no longer allure ?
And can we but sob, as such wrongs we endure,
    A's truagh gan oidhir 'n-a bh-farradh ?

Their famous, their holy, their dear Innis-Fail,
    A's truagh gan oidhir 'n-a bh-farradh!
Shall it be a prey for the stranger to spoil?
    A's truagh gan oidhir 'n-a bh-farradh!
Sure brave men would labor by night and by day
To banish that stranger away,
Or, dying for Ireland, the future would say
    A's truagh gan oidhir 'n-a bh-farradh!

Oh! shame—for unchanged is the face of our isle,
    A's truagh gan oidhir 'n-a bh-farradh!
That taught them to battle, to sing, and to smile,
    A's truagh gan oidhir 'n-a bh-farradh!
We are heirs of their rivers, their sea, and their land,
Our sky and our mountains as grand—
We are heirs—oh! we're not—of their heart and their hand,
    A's truagh gan oidhir 'n-a bh-farradh!

MUNSTER.

    Ye who rather
    Seek to gather
Biding thought than fleeting pleasure,
  In the South what wonders saw ye?
  From the South what lessons draw ye?
Wonders, passing thought or measure—
Lessons, through a life to treasure.

Ever living
Nature, giving
Welcome wild, or soft caress—
  Scenes that sink into the being,
  Till the eye grows full with seeing,
And the mute heart can but bless
Him that shaped such loveliness.

Dark and wide ill,
Rivers idle,
Wealth unwrought of sea and mine;
  Bays where Europe's fleet might anchor—
  Scarce Panama's waters blanker
Ere Columbus crossed the brine,
Void of living sound or sign.

God hath blest it,
Man opprest it—
Sad the fruits that mingling rise—
  Fallow fields, and hands to till them;
  Hungry mouths, and grain to fill them;
But a social curse denies
Labor's guerdon, want's supplies.

Sunlight glances,
Life that dances
In the limbs of childhood there—
  Glowing tints, that fade and sicken
  In the pallid, famine-stricken
Looks that men and women wear,
Living types of want and care.

>   Faith and patience
>   'Mid privations,
> Genial heart, and open hand;
>   But, what fain the eye would light on,
>   Pleasant homes to cheer and brighten
> Such a race and such a land—
> These, alas! their lords have banned.
>
>   These things press on
>   Us the lesson:
> Much may yet be done and borne;
>   But the bonds that thus continue
>   Paralyzing limb and sinew,
> From our country *must* be torn;
> Then shines out young Munster's morn.

SLIABH CUILINN.

THE TRUE IRISH KING.*

BY THOMAS DAVIS.

THE Cæsar of Rome has a wider demesne,
And the Ard-Righ of France has more clans in his train,
The sceptre of Spain is more heavy with gems,
And our crowns cannot vie with the Greek diadems;

---

* See Appendix L. to O'Donovan's "Hy-Fiachra," p. 245, &c.

But kinglier far, before heaven and man,
Are the emerald fields, and the fiery-eyed clan,
The sceptre, and state, and the poets who sing,
And the swords that encircle a TRUE IRISH KING!

For he must have come from a conquering race—
The heir of their valor, their glory, their grace:
His frame must be stately, his step must be fleet,
His hand must be trained to each warrior feat;
His face, as the harvest moon, steadfast and clear,
A head to enlighten, a spirit to cheer;
While the foremost to rush where the battle-brands ring,
And the last to retreat, is a TRUE IRISH KING!

Yet, not for his courage, his strength, or his name,
Can he from the clansmen their fealty claim.
The poorest and highest choose freely to-day
The chief, that to-night they'll as truly obey;
For loyalty springs from a people's consent,
And the knee that is forced had been better unbent—
The Sassanach serfs no such homage can bring
As the Irishman's choice of a TRUE IRISH KING!

Come, look on the pomp when they "make an O'Neill;"
The muster of dynasts—O'h-Again, O'Shiadhail,
O'Cathain, O'h-Anluain, O'Bhrislein and all,
From gentle Aird Uladh to rude Dun na n-gall:

K

"St. Patrick's *comharba*,"* with bishops thirteen,
And ollamhs, and breithams, and minstrels are seen
Round Tulach-Og† rath, like the bees in the spring,
All swarming to honor a TRUE IRISH KING!

Unsandalled he stands on the foot-dinted rock,
Like a pillar-stone fixed against every shock;
Round, round is the rath, on a far-seeing hill,
Like his blemishless honor and vigilant will.
The gray-beards are telling how chiefs by the score
Have been crowned on "The Rath of the Kings"
    heretofore;
While, crowded, yet ordered, within its green ring
Are the dynasts and priests round the TRUE IRISH
    KING!

The chronicler read him the laws of the clan,
And pledged him to bide by their blessing and ban;
His skian and his sword are unbuckled to show
That they only were meant for a foreigner foe;
A white willow wand has been put in his hand—
A type of pure, upright, and gentle command;
While hierarchs are blessing, the slipper they fling,
And O'Cathain proclaims him a TRUE IRISH KING!

Thrice looked he to heaven with thanks and with
    pray'r,
Thrice looked to his borders with sentinel stare,

---

* Successor—*comharba Phadraig*—the Archbishop of Armagh.
† In the county Tyrone, between Cookstown and Stewartstown.

To the waves of Loch N-Eathach, the heights of
    Strathbhan—
And thrice on his allies, and thrice on his clan.
One clash on their bucklers!—one more! they are
    still—
What means the deep pause on the crest of the
    hill?
Why gaze they above him?—a war-eagle's wing!
"'Tis an omen! Hurrah! for the TRUE IRISH
    KING!"

God aid him! God save him! and smile on his
    reign—
The terror of England, the ally of Spain.
May his sword be triumphant o'er Sassanach arts!
Be his throne ever girt by strong hands and true
    hearts!
May the course of his conquest run on till he see
The flag of Plantagenet sink in the sea,
And minstrels for ever his victories sing,
And saints make the bed of the TRUE IRISH KING.

THE GREEN FLAG.
A.D. 1647.
BY M. J. BARRY.

Boys! fill your glasses,
    Each hour that passes
Steals, it may be, on our last night's cheer.

The day soon shall come, boys,
 With fife and drum, boys,
Breaking shrilly on the soldier's ear.
Drink the faithful hearts that love us—
 'Mid to-morrow's thickest fight,
While our green flag floats above us,
 Think, boys, 'tis for them we smite.
  Down with each mean flag,
  None but the green flag
Shall above us be in triumph seen :
  Oh ! think on its glory,
  Long shrined in story,
Charge for Eire and her flag of green !

 Think on old Brian,
 War's mighty lion,
'Neath that banner 'twas he smote the Dane ;
 The Northman and Saxon
 Oft turned their backs on
Those who bore it o'er each crimsoned plain.
Beal-an-atha-Buidhe beheld it
 Bagenal's fiery onset curb ;
Scotch Munroe would fain have felled it—
 We, boys, followed him from red Beinnburb.
  Down with each mean flag,
  None but the green flag
Shall above us be in triumph seen :
  Oh ! think on its glory,
  Long shrined in story,
Charge with Eoghan for our flag of green !

    And if, at eve, boys,
    Comrades shall grieve, boys,
O'er our corses, let it be with pride,
    When thinking that each, boys,
    On that red beach, boys,
Lies the flood-mark of the battle's tide.
See! the first faint ray of morning
   Gilds the east with yellow light!
Hark! the bugle note gives warning—
   One full bumper to old friends to-night.
    Down with each mean flag,
    None but the green flag
Shall above us be in triumph seen:
    Oh! think on its glory,
    Long shrined in story,
Fall or conquer for our flag of green!

THE ISRAELITE LEADER.

A HEBREW youth, of thoughtful mien
   And dark, impassioned eye,
Once stood beside the leafy sheen
   Of an oak that towered high.
Ever, amid man's varied race,
   Such port and glance are found—
Unerring signs by which to trace
   The slave's first upward bound.

Ay! Liberty's good son, though he
   Yet bears the tyrant brand—
Not distant far the hour can be
   For such to arm and band.
His father's heaped-up corn was near,
   To tend it seemed his care;
But—souls like his to heaven are dear—
   An angel sought him there.

Under the shade of that tall oak
   A stranger met his eyes,
And glorious were the words he spoke
   Of Israel's quick uprise!
Deep, thrilling words—they instant made
   That young heart overflow,
As the strong leap of the cascade
   Heaves up the tide below.

He spread a feast for the harbinger
   Who such good tidings bore,
But fire from heaven consumed it there—
   He saw that guest no more;
And when the first deep awe had passed
   Of such strange visitant,
Up sprung his hopes for Israel, fast
   As eagles from their haunt.

And the pale youth who, but that morn
   (So meek of heart was he),
Stood winnowing his father's corn,
   At midnight, like a sea,

When tameless is its stormy roar,
    To Baal's high altar rushed,
And it was overturned before
    The next bright orient blushed.

An altar to the Living God
    Upon the ruin stood,
And groves where Baal's priests had trod
    Were rooted from the wood;
And God's good sword with Gideon went
    For ever from that day,
Till, of the hosts against him sent,
    Not one was left to slay.

Oh! names like his bright beacons are
    To realms that kings oppress,
Hailing, with radiant light from far,
    Their signals of distress.
When a crushed nation humbly turns
    From sin that was too dear,
Not long the proud oppressor spurns—
    Deliverance is near.

A———

RECRUITING SONG FOR THE IRISH BRIGADE.

BY MAURICE O'CONNELL.

Air—"*The White Cockade.*"

Is there a youthful gallant here
On fire for fame—unknowing fear—
Who, in the charge's mad career,
On Erin's foes would flesh his spear?
    Come, let him wear the white cockade,
    And learn the soldier's glorious trade;
    'Tis of such stuff a hero's made,
    Then let him join the bold Brigade.

Who scorns to own a Saxon lord,
And toil to swell a stranger's hoard?
Who, for rude blow or gibing word,
Would answer with the freeman's sword?
    Come, let him wear the white cockade, &c.

Does Erin's foully slandered name
Suffuse thy cheek with generous shame?
Wouldst right her wrongs—restore her fame?—
Come, then, the soldier's weapon claim—
    Come, then, and wear the white cockade, &c.

Come, free from bonds your father's faith,
Redeem its shrines from scorn and scathe—
The hero's fame, the martyr's wreath,
Will gild your life or crown your death.
    Then come, and wear the white cockade, &c.

To drain the cup—with girls to toy,
The serf's vile soul with bliss may cloy;
But wouldst thou taste a manly joy?—
Oh! it was ours at Fontenoy!
    Come, then, and wear the white cockade, &c.

To many a fight thy fathers led,
Full many a Saxon's life-blood shed;
From thee, as yet, no foe has fled—
Thou wilt not shame the glorious dead?
    Then come, and wear the white cockade, &c.

Oh! come—for slavery, want, and shame,
We offer vengeance, freedom, fame,
With monarchs comrade rank to claim,
And, nobler still, the patriot's name.
    Oh! come, and wear the white cockade,
    And learn the soldier's glorious trade;
    'Tis of such stuff a hero's made—
    Then come, and join the bold Brigade.

STEP TOGETHER.

BY M. J. BARRY.

Step together—boldly tread,
Firm each foot, erect each head,
Fixed in front be every glance—
Forward, at the word "advance"—
Serried files that foes may dread;
Like the deer on mountain heather,
    Tread light,
    Left, right—
Steady, boys, and step together!

Step together—be each rank
Dressed in line, from flank to flank,
Marching so that you may halt
'Mid the onset's fierce assault,
Firm as in the rampart's bank
Raised the iron rain to weather—
    Proud sight!
    Left, right—
Steady, boys, and step together!

Step together—be your tramp
Quick and light—no plodding stamp;
Let its cadence, quick and clear,
Fall like music on the ear;
Noise befits not hall or camp—

Eagles soar on silent feather ;
    Tread light,
    Left, right—
Steady, boys, and step together !

  Step together—self-restrained,
  Be your march of thought as trained.
  Each man's single powers combined
  Into one battalioned mind,
  Moving on with step sustained :
Thus prepared, we reck not whether
    Foes smite.
    Left, right—
We can think and strike together !

PATIENCE.

Be patient, oh! be patient! put your ear against the earth—
Listen there how noiselessly the germ o' the seed has birth,
How noiselessly and gently it upheaves its little way,
Till it parts the scarcely broken ground, and the blade stands forth to day.

Be patient, oh! be patient! for the germs of mighty thought

Must have their silent undergrowth, must underground be wrought;
But as sure as ever there's power that makes the grass appear,
Our land shall smile with liberty, the blade-time shall be here.

Be patient, oh! be patient! go and watch the wheat-ears grow
So imperceptibly that ye can mark nor change nor throe,
Day after day, day after day, till the ear is fully grown,
And then again, day after day, till the ripened field is brown.

Be patient, oh! be patient! though yet our hopes are green,
The harvest-fields of Freedom shall be crowned with sunny sheen.
Be ripening, be ripening, mature your silent way,
Till the whole broad land is tongued with fire on Freedom's harvest day.

SPARTACUS.

THE GREEN ABOVE THE RED.

BY THOMAS DAVIS.

Air—"*Irish Molly, O!*"

Full often, when our fathers saw the Red above the Green,
They rose in rude but fierce array, with sabre, pike, and skian,
And over many a noble town, and many a field of dead,
They proudly set the Irish Green above the English Red.

But in the end, throughout the land, the shameful sight was seen—
The English Red in triumph high above the Irish Green;
But well they died in breach and field, who, as their spirits fled,
Still saw the Green maintain its place above the English Red.

And they who saw, in after times, the Red above the Green,
Were withered as the grass that dies beneath a forest screen;

Yet often by this healthy hope their sinking hearts
    were fed,
That, in some day to come, the Green should flutter
    o'er the Red.

Sure 'twas for this Lord Edward died, and Wolfe
    Tone sunk serene—
Because they could not bear to leave the Red above
    the Green ;
And 'twas for this that Owen fought, and Sarsfield
    nobly bled—
Because their eyes were hot to see the Green above
    the Red.

So, when the strife began again, our darling Irish
    Green
Was down upon the earth, while high the English
    Red was seen ;
Yet still we held our fearless course, for something
    in us said,
"Before the strife is o'er you'll see the Green
    above the Red."

And 'tis for this we think and toil, and knowledge
    strive to glean,
That we may pull the English Red below the Irish
    Green,

And leave our sons sweet liberty, and smiling
    plenty spread
Above the land once dark with blood—*the Green
    above the Red !*

The jealous English tyrant now has banned the
    Irish Green,
And forced us to conceal it like a something foul
    and mean ;
But yet, by heavens ! he'll sooner raise his victims
    from the dead,
Than force our hearts to leave the Green and
    cotton to the Red !

We'll trust ourselves, for God is good, and blesses
    those who lean
On their brave hearts, and not upon an earthly
    king or queen ;
And, freely as we lift our hands, we vow our blood
    to shed,
Once and for evermore to raise the Green above
    the Red !

THE WELCOME.

BY THOMAS DAVIS.

Come in the evening, or come in the morning,
Come when you're looked for, or come without warning,
Kisses and welcome you'll find here before you,
And the oft'ner you come here the more I'll adore you.
  Light is my heart since the day we were plighted,
  Red is my cheek that they told me was blighted,
  The green of the trees looks far greener than ever,
  And the linnets are singing, "True lovers, don't sever!"

I'll pull you sweet flowers, to wear, if you choose them;
Or, after you've kissed them, they'll lie on my bosom.
I'll fetch from the mountain its breeze to inspire you;
I'll fetch from my fancy a tale that won't tire you
  Oh! your step's like the rain to the summer vexed farmer,
  Or sabre and shield to a knight without armor;
  I'll sing you sweet songs till the stars rise above me,
  Then, wandering, I'll wish you, in silence, to love me.

We'll look through the trees at the cliff and the
    eyrie;
We'll tread round the rath on the track of the
    fairy;
We'll look on the stars, and we'll list to the river,
Till you ask of your darling what gift you can give
    her.
    Oh! she'll whisper you, "Love as unchangeably
        beaming,
    And trust, when in secret, most tunefully stream-
        ing,
    Till the starlight of heaven above us shall quiver
    As our souls flow in one down eternity's river."

So come in the evening, or come in the morning,
Come when you're looked for, or come without
    warning,
Kisses and welcome you'll find here before you,
And the oft'ner you come here the more I'll adore
    you.
    Light is my heart since the day we were plighted,
    Red is my cheek that they told me was blighted,
    The green of the trees looks far greener than
        ever,
    And the linnets are singing, "True lovers, don't
        sever!"

WHY, GENTLES, WHY?

Air—"*Why, soldiers, why?*"

Why, gentles, why
Should we so melancholy be?
Why, gentles, why?
We know that all must die—
He, you, and I!
Life, at the best,
Is but a jest;
Hopes brightly shine but to fly.
Rejoice, then, that rest—
Deep, quiet, blest—
Stands ever nigh!

Why, tell me, why
Should we so melancholy be?
Why, tell me, why
Burst th' unbidden sigh,
While tears dim the eye?
Why crave for rest,
And, even when happiest,
Find gloomy thoughts ever nigh?
'Tis that while we live
Nought full content can give,
Known but on high!

L. N. F.

KATE OF ARAGLEN.

Air—"*An Cailin Ruadh.*"

BY DENNY LANE.

When first I saw thee, Kate, that summer evening late,
Down at the orchard gate of Araglen,
I felt I'd ne'er before seen one so fair, *a stór;*
I feared I'd never more see thee again.
I stopped and gazed at thee—my footfall, luckily,
Reached not thy ear, tho' we stood there so near;
While from thy lips a strain, soft as the summer rain,
Sad as a lover's pain, fell on my ear.

I've heard the lark in June, the harp's wild, plaintive tune,
The thrush, that aye too soon gives o'er his strain—
I've heard in hushed delight the mellow horn at night
Waking the echoes light of wild Loch Lein;
But neither echoing horn, nor thrush upon the thorn,
Nor lark at early morn hymning in air,
Nor harper's lay divine, e'er witched this heart of mine,
Like that sweet voice of thine, that evening there.

And when some rustling, dear, fell on thy listening ear,
You thought your brother near, and named his name,
I could not answer, though, as luck would have it so,
His name and mine, you know, were both the same;
Hearing no answering sound, you glanced in doubt around
With timid look, and found it was not he;
Turning away your head, and blushing rosy red,
Like a wild fawn you fled, far, far from me.

The swan upon the lake, the wild rose in the brake,
The golden clouds that make the west their throne,
The wild ash by the stream, the full moon's silver beam,
The evening star's soft gleam, shining alone;
The lily robed in white—all, all are fair and bright;
But ne'er on earth was sight so bright, so fair,
As that one glimpse of thee, that I caught then, *mo chree*,
It stole my heart from me that evening there.

And now you're mine alone, that heart is all my own—
That heart that ne'er hath known a flame before.

That form of mould divine, that snowy hand of thine,
Those locks of gold, are mine for evermore.
Was lover ever seen, as blest as thine, Kathleen?
Hath lover ever been more fond, more true?
Thine is my ev'ry vow! for ever dear, as now!
Queen of my heart be thou! *mo cailin ruadh !*

THE PILLAR TOWERS OF IRELAND.

BY D. F. M'CARTHY.

THE pillar towers of Ireland, how wondrously they stand
By the lakes and rushing rivers through the valleys of our land;
In mystic file, through the isle, they lift their heads sublime,
These gray old pillar temples—these conquerors of time!

Beside these gray old pillars, how perishing and weak
The Roman's arch of triumph, and the temple of the Greek,
And the gold domes of Byzantium, and the pointed Gothic spires—
All are gone, one by one, but the temples of our sires.

The column, with its capital, is level with the dust,
And the proud halls of the mighty and the calm
    homes of the just;
For the proudest works of man, as certainly, but
    slower,
Pass like the grass at the sharp scythe of the
    mower!

But the grass grows again when, in majesty and
    mirth,
On the wing of the Spring, comes the Goddess of
    the Earth;
But for man in this world no springtide e'er
    returns
To the labors of his hands or the ashes of his urns!

Two favorites hath Time—the pyramids of Nile,
And the old mystic temples of our own dear isle;
As the breeze o'er the seas, where the halcyon has
    its nest,
Thus time o'er Egypt's tombs and the temples of
    the West.

The names of their founders have vanished in the
    gloom,
Like the dry branch in the fire or the body in the
    tomb;
But to-day, in the ray, their shadows still they
    cast—
These temples of forgotten gods—these relics of
    the past!

Around these walls have wandered the Briton and
    the Dane,
The captives of Armorica, the cavaliers of Spain,
Phœnician and Milesian, and the plundering
    Norman peers,
And the swordsmen of brave Brian, and the chiefs
    of later years!

How many different rites have these gray old
    temples known!
To the mind what dreams are written in these
    chronicles of stone!
What terror and what error, what gleams of love
    and truth,
Have flashed from these walls since the world was
    in its youth!

Here blazed the sacred fire, and, when the sun was
    gone,
As a star from afar to the traveller it shone;
And the warm blood of the victim have these gray
    old temples drunk,
And the death-song of the druid and the matin of
    the monk.

Here was placed the holy chalice that held the
    sacred wine,
And the gold cross from the altar, and the relics
    from the shrine,

And the mitre shining brighter with its diamonds
    than the east,
And the crozier of the pontiff, and the vestments
    of the priest!

Where blazed the sacred fire, rung out the vesper
    bell;
Where the fugitive found shelter became the
    hermit's cell;
And hope hung out its symbol to the innocent and
    good,
For the cross o'er the moss of the pointed summit
    stood!

There may it stand for ever, while this symbol
    doth impart
To the mind one glorious vision, or one proud
    throb to the heart;
While the breast needeth rest may these gray old
    temples last,
Bright prophets of the future, as preachers of the
    past!

THE WILD GEESE.*

The wild geese—the wild geese—'tis long since
    they flew
O'er the billowy ocean's bright bosom of blue;
For the foot of the false-hearted stranger had curst
The shores on whose fond breast they'd settled at
    first;
And they sought them a home afar off o'er the sea,
Where their pinions, at least, might be chainless
    and free.

The wild geese—the wild geese—sad, sad was the
    wail
That followed their flight on the easterly gale;
But the eyes that had wept o'er their vanishing track
Ne'er brightened to welcome the wanderers back;
The home of their youth was the land of the slave,
And they died on that shore far away o'er the
    wave.

The wild geese—the wild geese—their coming once
    more
Was the long-cherished hope of that desolate
    shore,

---

* The recruits of the Irish Brigade were generally conveyed to France in the smugglers which brought foreign wines and brandy to our west coast, and were entered on the ships' books as "wild geese." Hence this became the common name for them among the country people.

For the loved ones behind knew it would yet be free,
If they flew on their white pinions back o'er the sea;
But vainly the hope of these lonely ones burned,
The wild geese—the wild geese—they never returned.

The wild geese—the wild geese—hark! heard ye that cry?
And marked ye that white flock o'erspreading the sky?
Can ye read not the omen? Joy, joy to the slave,
And gladness and strength to the hearts of the brave;
For wild geese are coming at length o'er the sea,
And Eirinn, green Eirinn, once more shall be free!

AID YOURSELVES AND GOD WILL AID YOU.

SIGNS and tokens round us thicken,
Hearts throb high and pulses quicken:
Comes the morn, though red and lurid—
   Clouds and storms around it hung—
Still it is that morn assured
   Long ye've prayed for, sought, and sung.
Soon those clouds may break, and render
To your noon its genial splendor—
Or in gloom more hopeless vest it;
On your heads the end is rested—
Front to front ye've now arrayed you,
Aid yourselves and God will aid you.

Awful, past all human telling,
Is the change upon you dwelling;
Act but now the fool or craven,
   And, like Canaan doomed of yore,
"Slave of slaves" shall be engraven
   On your foreheads evermore.
Crouching to your masters' mercies,
Drugged with slavery's cup like Circe's,
Scorn and by-word of the nations,
Curse of coming generations,
Blackest shame will overshade you—
Aid yourselves and God will aid you.

Hence, oh! hence such foul surmises!
Truer far a vision rises,
Men in Freedom's rank battalioned,
    Countless as the bristling grain,
Firm as ardent, wise as valiant,
    All to venture—all sustain;
Men of never-sinking patience,
Tried and taught by stern privations,
From their path nor lured nor driven,
Till their every bond is riven—
Every wrong dispersed like May dew—
Aid yourselves and God will aid you.

No! a heart-roused people's action
Cannot die like storms of faction.
Long a mute but master feeling
    In the millions' breast was nursed,
Till—a magic voice appealing—
    Forth it came, the thunder-burst!
'Gainst it now they plant their barriers,
Guard their keeps, and arm their warriors,
Lavish all their futile forces,
Power's most stale and vile resources,
Yet awhile to crush, degrade you:
Aid yourselves and God will aid you.

Blind misrule, and free opinion,
Armed lies, and truth's dominion,

In a battle still recurring
   Ever have these foes been set :
Here their deadliest strife is stirring—
   Who can doubt the issue yet ?
Watch and wait, your hour abiding,
Nought your goal one moment hiding,
Fearing not, nor too confiding,
Trusting in your leader's guiding—
His who ne'er forsook, betrayed you :
Aid yourselves and God will aid you.

But, should all be unavailing—
Reason, truth, and justice failing,
Every peaceful effort blighted,
   Every shred of freedom reft—
Then—oh ! are we crushed or frighted
   While one remedy is left ?
Back ! each slave that faints or falters;
On ! true heart that never alters ;
On ! stout arm no terrors weaken,
Bruce's star and Tell's your beacon ;
Strike—that stroke is many a day due :
Aid yourselves and God will aid you.

                      SLIABH CUILINN.

WATCH AND WAIT.

BY CHARLES GAVAN DUFFY.

Air—"*Tow row row.*"

Sadly, as a muffled drum,
  Toll the hours of long probation:
Let them toll, the stable soul
  Can work and wait to build a nation.
      Curse or groan
     Never more shall own
  But our stifled hearts are patient
     As a stone.

Yes, as patient as a stone,
  Till we're struck in hate or ire;
Then the dint will fall on flint,
  And send them back a stream of fire!
      Wait, boys, wait,
     Ready for your fate,
  Prompt as powder to the linstock
     Soon or late!

Let us gather love and help,
  Won from native friends and foemen;
How little loath the hearts of both,
  We read in many a glorious omen.
      No, boys, no,
     Let no word or blow
  Brand a native Irish brother
     As our foe.

Holy Freedom's pealing voice
    Willing slaves hath never woken;
Ireland's trance was ignorance,
    And KNOWLEDGE all her spells hath broken.
        Hell and night
        Vanish from her sight,
As when God pronounced aforetime,
        " Be there light!"

Cherish well this sacred flame,
    Feed its lamp with care and patience;
From God it came, its destined aim
    To burst the fetters off the nations.
        Now, boys, now,
        Why should we bow,
When the promised day is dawning,
        And that's *now* ?

Brothers, if this day should set,
    Another yet must crown our freedom;
That will come with roll of drum
    And trampling files with MEN to lead them
        Who can save
        Renegade or slave?
Fortune only twines her garlands
        For the brave!

CLARE'S DRAGOONS.

BY THOMAS DAVIS.

Air—"*Viva la.*"

When on Ramillies' bloody field
The baffled French were forced to yield,
The victor Saxon backward reeled
   Before the charge of Clare's Dragoons.
The flags we conquered in that fray
Look lone in Ypres' choir, they say;
We'll win them company to-day,
   Or bravely die like Clare's Dragoons.

CHORUS.

   Viva la for Ireland's wrong!
     Viva la for Ireland's right!
   Viva la in battle throng
     For a Spanish steed and sabre bright.

The brave old lord died near the fight,
But, for each drop he lost that night,
A Saxon cavalier shall bite
   The dust before Lord Clare's Dragoons.
For never, when our spurs were set,
And never when our sabres met,
Could we the Saxon soldiers get
   To stand the shock of Clare's Dragoons.

CHORUS.

Viva la the New Brigade!
  Viva la the Old One, too!
Viva la, the Rose shall fade,
  And the Shamrock shine for ever new!

Another Clare is here to lead,
The worthy son of such a breed;
The French expect some famous deed
  When Clare leads on his bold Dragoons.
Our colonel comes from Brian's race,
His wounds are in his breast and face,
The *bearna baeghail** is still his place,
  The foremost of his bold Dragoons.

CHORUS.

Viva la the New Brigade!
  Viva la the Old One too!
Viva la, the Rose shall fade,
  And the Shamrock shine for ever new.

There's not a man in squadron here
Was ever known to flinch or fear,
Though first in charge and last in rear
  Have ever been Lord Clare's Dragoons.

---

* The gap of danger.

But, see! we'll soon have work to do,
To shame our boasts, or prove them true,
For hither comes the English crew
   To sweep away Lord Clare's Dragoons!

CHORUS.

Viva la for Ireland's wrong!
   Viva la for Ireland's right!
Viva la in battle throng
   For a Spanish steed and sabre bright!

O comrades! think how Ireland pines,
Her exiled lords, her rifled shrines,
Her dearest hope the ordered lines
   And bursting charge of Clare's Dragoons.
Then fling your Green Flag to the sky,
Be Limerick your battle-cry,
And charge till blood floats fetlock high
   Around the track of Clare's Dragoons.

CHORUS.

Viva la the New Brigade!
   Viva la the Old One, too!
Viva la, the Rose shall fade,
   And the Shamrock shine for ever new!

THE PATRIOT BRAVE.

BY R. D. WILLIAMS.

I DRINK to the valiant who combat
   For freedom by mountain or wave;
And may triumph attend, like a shadow,
   The swords of the patriot brave!
Oh! never was holier chalice
   Than this at our festivals crowned—
The heroes of Morven, to pledge it,
   And gods of Valhalla, float round.
      Hurrah for the patriot brave!
      A health to the patriot brave!
And a curse and a blow be to liberty's foe,
      Whether tyrant, or coward, or knave.

Great spirits, who battled in old time
   For the freedom of Athens, descend!
As low to the shadow of Brian
   In fond hero-worship we bend.
From those that in far Alpine passes
   Saw Dathi struck down in his mail,
To the last of our chiefs' galloglasses,
   The saffron-clad foes of the Pale,
      Let us drink to the patriot brave;
      Hurrah for the patriot brave!
But a curse and a blow be to liberty's foe,
      And more chains for the satisfied slave.

O Liberty! hearts that adore thee
  Pour out their best blood at thy shrine,
As freely as gushes before thee
  This purple libation of wine.
For us, whether destined to triumph,
  Or bleed as Leonidas bled,
Crushed down by a forest of lances
  On mountains of foreigner dead,
    May we sleep with the patriot brave!
    God prosper the patriot brave!
But may battle and woe hurry liberty's foe
  To a bloody and honorless grave!

THE FALL OF THE LEAVES.

BY THE REV. C. MEEHAN.

I.

They are falling, they are falling, and soon, alas! they'll fade,
The flowers of the garden, the leaves of dell and glade;
Their dirge the winds are singing in the lone and fitful blast,
And the leaves and flowers of summer are strewn and fading fast.

Ah! why, then, have we loved them, when their
    beauties might have told
They could not linger long with us, nor stormy
    skies behold?
Fair creatures of the sunshine! your day of life
    is past,
Ye are scattered by the rude winds, fallen and
    fading fast:
And, oh! how oft enchanted have we watched your
    opening bloom,
When you made unto the day-god your offerings of
    perfume!
How vain our own imaginings that joy will always
    last—
'Tis like to you, ye sweet things, all dimmed and
    faded fast.
The glens where late ye bloomed for us are leafless
    now and lorn,
The tempest's breath hath all their pride and all
    their beauty shorn.

II.

'Twas ever so, and so shall be—by fate that doom
    was cast—
The things we love are scarcely seen till they are
    gone and past.
Ay, ye are gone and faded, ye leaves and lovely
    flowers,
But when spring comes you'll come again to deck
    the garden's bowers;

And beauty, too, will cull you, and twine ye in her
    hair—
What meeter, truer emblem can beauty ever
    wear?
But never here, oh! never shall we the loved ones
    meet
Who shone in youth around us, and, like you,
    faded fleet;
Full soon affliction bowed them, and life's day-
    dawn o'ercast—
They're blooming now in heaven, their day of
    fading's past!
Ye withered leaves and flowers! oh! may you
    long impart
Monition grave and moral stern unto this erring
    heart—
Oh! teach it that the joys of earth are short-lived,
    vain, and frail,
And transient as the leaves and flowers before the
    wintry gale.

CATE OF CEANN-MARE.*

BY D. F. M'CARTHY.

I.

Oh! many bright eyes full of goodness and gladness,
   Where the pure soul looks out and the heart loves to shine,
And many cheeks pale with the soft hue of sadness,
   Have I worshipped in silence and felt them divine!
But hope in its gleamings, or love in its dreamings,
   Ne'er fashioned a being so faultless and fair
As the lily-cheeked beauty, the rose of the Ruachtach,†
   The fawn of the valley, sweet Cate of Ceannmare!

II.

It was all but a moment, her radiant existence,
   Her presence, her absence, all crowded on me;
But time has not ages, and earth has not distance,
   To sever, sweet vision, my spirit from thee!
Again am I straying where children are playing,
   Bright is the sunshine and balmy the air,
Mountains are heathy, and there do I see thee,
   Sweet fawn of the valley, young Cate of Ceannmare!

---

* Properly Ceann-Mara—head of the sea
† Commonly written Roughty.

III.

Thy own bright arbutus hath many a cluster
   Of white, flaxen blossoms, like lilies in air,
But, oh! thy pale cheek hath a delicate lustre
   No blossoms can rival, no lily doth wear.
To that cheek softly flushing, to thy lip brightly
     blushing,
   Oh! what are the berries that bright tree doth
     bear?
Peerless in beauty, the rose of the Ruachtach,
   That fawn of the valley, sweet Cate of Ceann-mare!

IV.

O beauty! some spell from kind nature thou
     bearest,
   Some magic of tone or enchantment of eye,
That hearts that are hardest from forms that are
     fairest
   Receive such impressions as never can die.
The foot of the fairy, though lightsome and airy,
   Can stamp on the hard rock the shape it doth
     wear;
Art cannot trace it, nor ages efface it—
   And such are thy glances, sweet Cate of Ceann-
     mare!

V.

To him who far travels how sad is the feeling,
   How the light of his mind is o'ershadowed and
     dim,

When the scenes he most loves, like the river's
    soft stealing,
  All fade as a vision, and vanish from him!
Yet he bears from each far land a flower for that
    garland
  That memory weaves of the bright and the fair;
While this sigh I am breathing *my* garland is
    wreathing,
  And the rose of that garland is Cate of Ceann-
    mare!

VI.

In lonely Lough Quinlan,* in summer's soft hours,
  Fair islands are floating that move with the tide,
Which, sterile at first, are soon covered with
    flow'rs,
  And thus o'er the bright waters fairy-like glide!
Thus the mind the most vacant is quickly
    awakened,
  And the heart bears a harvest that late was so
    bare,
Of him who, in roving, finds objects in loving
  Like the fawn of the valley, sweet Cate of
    Ceann-mare!

---

* Dr. Smith, in his "History of Kerry," says: "Near this place is a considerable fresh-water lake, called Lough Quinlan, in which are some small floating islands, much admired by the country people. These islands swim from side to side of the lake, and are usually composed at first of a long kind of grass, which being blown off the adjacent grounds about the middle of September, and floating about, collect slime and other stuff, and so yearly increase till they come to have grass and other vegetables grown upon them."

Sweet Cate of Ceann mare! though I ne'er may
    behold thee—
Though the pride and the joy of another you be—
Though strange lips may praise thee and strange
    arms enfold thee,
  A blessing, dear Cate, be on them and on thee!
One feeling I cherish that never can perish—
  One talisman proof to the dark wizard, Care—
The fervent and dutiful love of the beautiful,
  Of which *thou* art a type, gentle Cate of Ceann-
    mare!

A LAY SERMON.

BY CHARLES GAVAN DUFFY.

I.

Brother, do you love your brother?
    Brother, are you all you seem?
Do you live for more than living?
    Has your life a law and scheme?
Are you prompt to bear its duties,
    As a brave man may beseem?

II.

Brother, shun the mist exhaling
    From the fen of pride and doubt;
Neither seek the house of bondage,
    Walling straitened souls about—
Bats! who, from their narrow spy-hole,
    Cannot see a world without.

III.

Anchor in no stagnant shallow;
    Trust the wide and wondrous sea,
Where the tides are fresh for ever,
    And the mighty currents free:
There, perchance, O young Columbus!
    Your New World of truth may be.

IV.

Favor will not make deserving—
    (Can the sunshine brighten clay?)—
Slowly must it grow to blossom,
    Fed by labor and delay;
And the fairest bud of promise
    Bears the taint of quick decay.

V.

You must strive for better guerdons—
    Strive to *be* the thing you'd seem;
Be the thing that God hath made you,
    Channel for no borrowed stream;
He hath lent you mind and conscience—
    See you travel in their beam!

VI.

See you scale life's misty highlands
    By this light of living truth!

And, with bosom braced for labor,
    Breast them in your manly youth;
So, when age and care have found you,
    Shall your downward path be smooth.

VII.

Fear not, on that rugged highway,
    Life may want its lawful zest;
Sunny glens are in the mountain,
    Where the weary feet may rest,
Cooled in streams that gush for ever
    From a loving mother's breast.

VIII.

"Simple heart and simple pleasures,"
    So they write life's golden rule.
Honor won by supple baseness,
    State that crowns a cankered fool,
Gleam as gleam the gold and purple
    On a hot and rancid pool.

IX.

Wear no show of wit or science,
    But the gems you've won and weighed
Thefts, like ivy on a ruin,
    Make the rifts they seem to shade:
Are you not a thief and beggar
    In the rarest spoils arrayed?

X.

Shadows deck a sunny landscape,
  Making brighter all the bright;
So, my brother! care and danger
  On a loving nature light,
Bringing all its latent beauties
  Out upon the common sight.

XI.

Love the things that God created,
  Make your brother's need your care;
Scorn and hate repel God's blessings,
  But where love is, *they* are there;
As the moonbeams light the waters,
  Leaving rock and sand-bank bare.

XII.

Thus, my brother, grow and flourish,
  Fearing none and loving all;
For the true man needs no patron—
  He shall climb, and never crawl;
Two things fashion their own channel—
  The strong man and the waterfall.

THE BISHOP OF ROSS.

BY DR. MADDEN,

Author of the "Lives of the United Irishmen."

I.

The tramp of the trooper is heard at Macroom ;*
    The soldiers of Cromwell are spared from Clonmel,†
And Broghill—the merciless Broghill—is come
    On a mission of murder which pleases him well.

II.

The wailing of women, the wild *ulula*,
    Dread tidings from cabin to cabin convey;
But loud though the plaints and the shrieks which ensue,
    The war-cry is louder of men in array.

III.

In the park of Macroom there is gleaming of steel,
    And glancing of lightning in looks on that field,
And swelling of bosoms with patriot zeal,
    And clenching of hands on the weapons they wield.

* Magh Cromha.   † Cluain Meala.

IV.

MacEgan,* a prelate like Ambrose of old,
    Forsakes not his flock when the spoiler is near;
The post of the pastor's in front of the fold
    When the wolf's on the plain and there's rapine to fear.

V.

The danger is come, and the fortune of war
    Inclines to the side of oppression once more;
The people are brave—but, they fall; and the star
    Of their destiny sets in the darkness of yore.

VI.

MacEgan survives in the Philistine hands
    Of the lords of the Pale, and his death is decreed;
But the sentence is stayed by Lord Broghill's commands,
    And the prisoner is dragged to his presence with speed.

VII.

"To Carraig-an-Droichid† this instant," he cried,
    "Prevail on your people in garrison there
To yield, and at once in our mercy confide,
    And your life I will pledge you my honor to spare."

---

* Mac Aodhagain in proper spelling.

† Commonly written Carrigadrohid (the Rock of the Bridge), three miles east of Macroom, county Cork. The castle is built on a steep rock in the river Lee, by the M'Carthys.

VIII.

" *Your mercy! your honor!* " the prelate replied,
    "I well know the worth of: my duty I know,
Lead on to the castle, and there, by your side,
    With the blessing of God, what is meet will I do."

IX.

The orders are given, the prisoner is led
    To the castle, and round him are menacing
        hordes :
Undaunted, approaching the walls, at the head
    Of the troopers of Cromwell, he utters these
        words :

X.

" Beware of the cockatrice—trust not the wiles
    Of the serpent, for perfidy skulks in its folds !
Beware of Lord Broghill the day that he smiles !
    His mercy is murder !—his word never holds.

XI.

" Remember, 'tis writ in our annals of blood,
    Our countrymen never relied on the faith
Of truce, or of treaty, but treason ensued—
    And the issue of every delusion was death !"

XII.

Thus nobly the patriot prelate sustained
    The ancient renown of his chivalrous race,
And the last of old Eoghan's descendants obtained
    For the name of Ui-Mani new lustre and grace.

XIII.

He died on the scaffold, in front of those walls
 Where the blackness of ruin is seen from afar;
And the gloom of its desolate aspect recalls
 The blackest of Broghill's achievements in war!

OUR OWN AGAIN.

BY THOMAS DAVIS.

I.

Let the coward shrink aside,
 We'll have our own again;
Let the brawling slave deride,
 Here's for our own again;
Let the tyrant bribe and lie,
March, threaten, fortify,
Loose his lawyer and his spy,
 Yet we'll have our own again.
Let him soothe in silken tone,
Scold from a foreign throne,
Let him come with bugles blown,
 We shall have our own again.
Let us to our purpose bide,
 We'll have our own again;
Let the game be fairly tried,
 We'll have our own again.

II.

Send the cry throughout the land,
  "Who's for our own again?"
Summon all men to our band,
  Why not our own again?
Rich, and poor, and old, and young,
Sharp sword, and fiery tongue,
Soul, and sinew firmly strung,
  All to get our own again.
Brothers thrive by brotherhood—
Trees in a stormy wood—
Riches come from nationhood—
  Sha'n't we have our own again?
Munster's woe is Ulster's bane—
  Join for our own again;
Tyrants rob as well as reign—
  We'll have our own again.

III.

Oft our fathers' hearts it stirred,
  "Rise for our own again!"
Often passed the signal word,
  "Strike for our own again!"
Rudely, rashly, and untaught,
Uprose they, ere they ought,
Failing, though they nobly fought,
  Dying for their own again.
Mind will rule and muscle yield
In senate, ship, and field—

When we've skill our strength to wield,
    Let us take our own again.
By the slave his chain is wrought—
    Strive for our own again;
Thunder is less strong than thought—
    We'll have our own again.

IV.

Calm as granite to our foes,
    Stand for our own again,
Till his wrath to madness grows—
    Firm for our own again.
Bravely hope and wisely wait,
Toil, join, and educate;
Man is master of his fate;
    We'll enjoy our own again.
With a keen, constrained thirst—
Powder's calm ere it burst—
Making ready for the worst,
    So we'll get our own again.
Let us to our purpose bide,
    We'll have our own again;
God is on the righteous side,
    We'll have our own again.

A PATRIOT'S HAUNTS.

BY WILLIAM P. MULCHINECK.

I LOVE the mountain rude and high,
Its bare and barren majesty,
And in its peopled solitude
I love to stand in musing mood,
And bring, by fancy's magic pow'r,
Bright dreams to charm the passing hour.
To fill the green and heathy glen
With hosts of stalwart fighting men,
With banners flaunting fair and free,
Fit for a new Thermopylæ;
And in the dark and narrow pass
I place a young Leonidas.
With joy I mark the phantom fight,
And hear the shouts for native right;
And thus, until the shades of night
Proclaim time's quick and restless flight,
In fancy, freedom's war I see,
And tread a land by slaves made free.

I love to mark the billows rise,
And fling their spray into the skies—
To mark the bold, impetuous shock
They deal upon the rugged rock;
Until, where'er its side they lave,
Their power is shown in many a cave.

I match the rock to tyranny,
The waves to slaves and man made free;
For know, 'twas unity like this
That Greece put forth at Salamis;
And thus the Romans, side by side,
From Carthage tore her crest of pride;
And yet, where slaves are found, I ween,
New Fabii may still be seen,
Whose hearts, though bold enough, I trow,
See not the fitting moment now—
Can find not yet the unity
That made the Doric children free,
That made the haughty Samnite fly
The anger of a Roman eye.

Doubters! ascend a mountain-height,
With healthy pulse and sinew light—
Cowards! upon the foaming tide
Cast your glances, far and wide,
And in the dark hill say with me,
" There's many a sure Thermopylæ,"
And o'er each bay's profound abyss,
" True hearts could make a Salamis."

A HEALTH.

BY J. D. FRAZER.

I.

Hurrah! our feuds are drowned at last;
   Hurrah! let tyrants tremble;
The fronted foemen of the past
   In brotherhood assemble.
Fill up—and with a lofty tongue
   As ever spoke from steeple,
From shore to shore *his* health be rung—
   The leader of the people.

II.

In mighty triumphs, singly won,
   The nation has a token
That mightier deeds will yet be done—
   The last strong fetter broken;
Since hearts of nerve and hands of strength,
   Once banded to resist him,
Unfurl his flag, and share at length
   The glory to assist him.

III.

Up with the wine from boss to brim,
   And be his voice the loudest
Who rears, at risk of life or limb,
   Our country's flag the proudest.

"*The leader of the people*"—grand,
   Yet simple wisdom guide him!
And glory to the men who stand,
   Like sheathed swords, beside him.

ORANGE AND GREEN WILL CARRY THE DAY.

BY THOMAS DAVIS.

Air—"*The Protestant Boys.*"

I.

Ireland! rejoice, and England! deplore,
   Faction and feud are passing away.
'Twas a low voice, but 'tis a loud roar,
   "Orange and Green will carry the day."
      Orange! Orange!
      Green and Orange!
Pitted together in many a fray—
      Lions in fight!
      And, linked in their might,
Orange and Green will carry the day.
      Orange! Orange!
      Green and Orange!
Wave them together o'er mountain and bay,
      Orange and Green!
      Our king and our queen!
Orange and Green will carry the day!

II.

Rusty the swords our fathers unsheathed ;
  William and James are turned to clay ;
Long did we till the wrath they bequeathed—
  Red was the crop, and bitter the pay !
      Freedom fled us !
      Knaves misled us !
Under the feet of the foemen we lay ;
      Riches and strength
      We'll win them at length,
For Orange and Green will carry the day !
      Landlords fooled us,
      England ruled us,
Hounding our passions to make us their prey :
      But, in their spite,
      The Irish " unite,"
And Orange and Green will carry the day !

III.

Fruitful our soil where honest men starve,
  Empty the mart, and shipless the bay ;
Out of our want the oligarchs carve ;
  Foreigners fatten on our decay !
      Disunited,
      Therefore blighted,
Ruined and rent by the Englishman's sway ,
      Party and creed
      For once have agreed—
Orange and Green will carry the day !

Boyne's old water,
Red with slaughter,
Now is as pure as an infant at play;
So in our souls
Its history rolls,
And Orange and Green will carry the day!

IV.

English deceit can rule us no more;
  Bigots and knaves are scattered like spray,
Deep was the oath the Orangeman swore,
  "Orange and Green must carry the day!"
Orange! Orange!
Bless the Orange!
Tories and Whigs grew pale with dismay,
When from the North
Burst the cry forth,
"Orange and Green will carry the day!"
No surrender!
No pretender!
Never to falter and never betray—
With an Amen
We swear it again,
Orange and Green shall carry the day!

A HIGHWAY FOR FREEDOM.

BY CLARENCE MANGAN.

Air.—"*Boyne Water.*"

I.

"My suffering country shall be freed,
    And shine with tenfold glory!"
So spake the gallant Winkelried,
    Renowned in German story.
"No tyrant, even of kingly grade,
    Shall cross or darken *my* way!"
Out flashed his blade, and so he made
    For Freedom's course a highway!

II.

We want a man like this, with pow'r
    To rouse the world by *one* word;
We want a chief to meet the hour,
    And march the masses onward.
But, chief or none, through blood and fire,
    My fatherland, lies *thy* way!
The men must fight who dare desire
    For Freedom's course a highway!

III.

Alas! I can but idly gaze
    Around in grief and wonder,
The people's will alone can raise
    The people's shout of thunder.

Too long, my friends, you faint for fear,
    In secret crypt and by-way;
At last be men! Stand forth and clear
    For Freedom's course a highway!

IV.

You intersect wood, lea, and lawn,
    With roads for monster wagons,
Wherein you speed like lightning, drawn
    By fiery iron dragons.
So do. Such work is good, no doubt;
    But why not seek some nigh way
For *mind* as well? Path also out
    For Freedom's course a highway!

V.

Yes! up! and let your weapons be
    Sharp steel and self-reliance!
Why waste your burning energy
    In void and vain defiance,
And phrases fierce but fugitive?
    'Tis deeds, not words, that *I* weigh—
Your swords and guns alone can give
    To Freedom's course a highway!

ADVANCE.

BY D. F. M‘CARTHY.

God bade the sun with golden step sublime
                            Advance!
He whispered in the listening ear of time,
                            Advance!
He bade the guiding spirits of the stars,
With lightning speed, in silver, shining cars,
Along the bright floor of his azure hall
                            Advance!
Sun, stars, and time obey the voice, and all
                            Advance!
The river at its bubbling fountain cries
                            Advance!
The clouds proclaim, like heralds through the skies,
                            Advance!
Throughout the world the mighty Master's laws
Allow not one brief moment's idle pause:
The earth is full of life, the swelling seeds
                            Advance!
The summer hours, like flow'ry harnessed steeds,
                            Advance!
To man's most wondrous hand the same voice cried,
                            Advance!
Go draw the marble from its secret bed,
And make the cedar bend its giant head;

Let domes and columns through the wondering air
                                      Advance!
The world, O man! is thine. But wouldst thou share—
                                      Advance!
Go, track the comet in its wheeling race,
And drag the lightning from its hiding place;
From out the night of ignorance and fears
                                      Advance!
For love and hope, borne by the coming years,
                                      Advance!
All heard, and some obeyed the great command,
                                      Advance!
It passed along from listening land to land—
                                      Advance!
The strong grew stronger, and the weak grew strong,
As passed the war-cry of the world along;
Awake, ye nations! know your powers and rights—
                                      Advance!
Through hope and work, to freedom's new delights
                                      Advance!
Knowledge came down and waved his steady torch—
                                      Advance!
Sages proclaim, 'neath many a marble porch,
                                      Advance!

As rapid lightning leaps from peak to peak,
The Gaul, the Goth, the Roman, and the
    Greek,
The painted Briton, caught the winged word,
                               Advance!
And earth grew young, and carolled, as a bird,
                               Advance!
O Ireland! oh, my country! wilt thou not
                               Advance?
Wilt thou not share the world's progressive
    lot?
                               Advance!
Must seasons change, and countless years roll
    on,
And thou remain a darksome Ajalon,
And never see the crescent moon of hope?
                               Advance!
'Tis time thine heart and eye had wider scope—
                               Advance!
Dear brothers, wake! look up! be firm! be
    strong!
From out the starless night of fraud and wrong
                               Advance!
The chains have fallen from off thy wasted
    hands,
And every man a seeming freeman stands;
But, ah! 'tis in the soul that freedom dwells—
                               Advance!
Proclaim that *there* thou wearest no manacles—
                               Advance!

Advance!—thou must advance or perish now—
        Advance!
Advance! Why live with wasted heart and brow?
        Advance!
Advance! or sink at once into the grave;
Be bravely free, or artfully a slave.
Why fret thy master, if thou must have one?
        Advance!
Advance three steps, the glorious work is done—
        Advance!
The first is courage—'tis a giant stride!
        Advance!
With bounding step, up Freedom's rugged side,
        Advance!
Knowledge will lead you to the dazzling heights;
Tolerance will teach and guard your brother's rights.
Faint not! for thee a pitying future waits!
        Advance!
Be wise, be just, with will as fixed as Fate's
        Advance!

THE IRISH ARMS BILL.

BY WILLIAM DRENNAN.

I.

My country, alas! we may blush for thee now,
The brand of the slave broadly stamped on thy
    brow!
Unarmed must thy sons and thy daughters await
The Sassenagh's lust or the Sassenagh's hate.

II.

Through the length and the breadth of thy regions
    they roam;
Many huts and some halls may be there—but no
    home;
Rape and Murder cry out, "Let each door be
    unbarred!
Deliver your arms, and then stand on your guard!"

III.

For England hath wakened at length from her
    trance—
She might knuckle to Russia, and truckle to
    France,
And, licking the dust from America's feet,
Might vow she had ne'er tasted sugar so sweet.

IV.

She could leave her slain thousands, her captives,
    in pawn,
And, Akhbar to lord it o'er Affghanistan,
And firing the village or rifling the ground
Of the poor, murdered peasant, slink off like a
    hound.

V.

What then? She can massacre wretched Chinese,
Can rob the ameers of their lands, if she please,
And when Hanover wrings from her duties not
    due,
She can still vent her wrath, enslaved Erin! on you.

VI.

Thus—but why, beloved land, longer sport with
    thy shame?
If my life could wipe out the foul blot from thy
    fame,
How gladly for thee were this spirit outpoured,
On the scaffold as free as by shot or by sword!

VII.

Yet, oh! in fair field, for one soldier-like blow,
To fall in thy cause, or look far for thy foe;
To sleep on thy bosom, down-trodden with thee,
Or to wave in thy breeze the green flag of the free!

o

VIII.

Heaven! to think of the thousands far better
    than I,
Who for thee, sweetest mother, would joyfully die!
Then to reckon the insult—the rapine—the wrong!
How long, God of love?—God of battles! how
    long?

MY GRAVE.

BY THOMAS DAVIS.

Shall they bury me in the deep,
Where wind-forgetting waters sleep?
Shall they dig a grave for me
Under the green-wood tree?
Or on the wild heath,
Where the wilder breath
Of the storm doth blow?
Oh, no! oh, no!

Shall they bury me in the palace tombs,
Or under the shade of cathedral domes?
Sweet 'twere to lie on Italy's shore;
Yet not there—nor in Greece, though I love it
    more.
In the wolf or the vulture my grave shall I find?
Shall my ashes career on the world-seeing wind?

Shall they fling my corpse in the battle mound,
Where coffinless thousands lie under the ground—
Just as they fall they are buried so?
Oh, no! oh, no!

No! on an Irish green-hill side,
On an opening lawn, but not too wide!
For I love the drip of the wetted trees;
I love not the gales, but a gentle breeze
To freshen the turf; put no tombstone there,
But green sods, decked with daisies fair;
Nor sods too deep, but so that the dew
The matted grass-roots may trickle through.
Be my epitaph writ on my country's mind:
"He served his country, and loved his kind."
Oh! 'twere merry unto the grave to go,
If one were sure to be buried so.

THE VOW OF TIPPERARY.

BY THOMAS DAVIS.

Air—"*The Men of Tipperary.*"

I.

From Carrick streets to Shannon shore—
From Sliabh na m-Ban* to Ballindeary—
From Longford Pass to Gaillte Mor—
Come hear the vow of Tipperary.

* Commonly written Slievenamon.

II.

Too long we fought for Britain's cause,
And of our blood were never chary;
She paid us back with tyrant laws,
And thinned the homes of Tipperary.

III.

Too long, with rash and single arm,
The peasant strove to guard his eyrie,
Till Irish blood bedewed each farm,
And Ireland wept for Tipperary.

IV.

But never more we'll lift a hand—
We swear by God and Virgin Mary!—
Except in war for native land;
And *that's* the Vow of Tipperary!

ENGLAND'S ULTIMATUM.

" Repeal must not be argued with. Were the Union gall it must be maintained. Ireland must have England as her sister, or her subjugatrix. This is our ultimatum."—Times.

I.

SLAVES! lie down and kiss your chains,
  To the Union yield in quiet;
Were it hemlock in your veins,
  Stand it must—*we* profit by it.

II.

English foot on Irish neck,
  English gyve on Irish sinew,
Ireland swayed at England's beck—
  So it is, and shall continue.

III.

English foot on Irish neck,
  Pine or rot, meanwhile, we care not;
Little will we pause to reck
  How you writhe, while rise you dare not.

IV.

Argue with you!—stoop to show
  Our dominion's just foundation!
Savage Celts! and dare you so
  Task the lords of half creation?

V.

Argue! do not ask again,
   Proofs enough there are to sway you,
Three-and-twenty thousand men,
   Whom a word will loose to slay you.

VI.

Store of arguments besides
   In their time we will exhibit—
Leaded thongs for rebel hides,
   Flaming thatch, and burthened gibbet.

VII.

Bid your fathers tell how we
   Proved our rights in bygone seasons;
Slaves! and sons of slaves!—your knee
   Bow to *sister* England's reasons.

SLIABH CUILINN.

FONTENOY.

BY THOMAS DAVIS.

I.

THRICE at the huts of Fontenoy the English column failed,
And twice the lines of St. Antoine the Dutch in vain assailed;
For town and slope were guarded with fort and artillery,
And well they swept the English ranks and Dutch auxiliary.
As vainly through De Barri's wood the British soldiers burst,
The French artillery drove them back, diminished and dispersed.
The bloody Duke of Cumberland beheld with anxious eye,
And ordered up his last reserve, his latest chance to try.
On Fontenoy, on Fontenoy, how fast his generals ride!
And mustering come his chosen troops, like clouds at eventide.

II.

Six thousand English veterans in stately column tread,
Their cannon blaze in front and flank, Lord Hay is at their head;

Steady they step a-down the slope—steady they
    climb the hill—
Steady they load—steady they fire, moving right
    onward still
Betwixt the wood and Fontenoy, as through a
    furnace blast,
Through rampart, trench, and palisade, and bullets
    show'ring fast;
And on the open plain above they rose, and kept
    their course,
With ready fire and steadiness, that mocked at
    hostile force.
Past Fontenoy, past Fontenoy, while thinner grow
    their ranks,
They break, as broke the Zuyder Zee through
    Holland's ocean banks.

III.

More idly than the summer flies French tirailleurs
    rush round;
As stubble to the lava tide, French squadrons
    strew the ground;
Bombshell, and grape, and round shot tore, still
    on they marched and fired—
Fast from each volley grenadier and voltigeur
    retired.
"Push on, my household cavalry," King Louis
    madly cried:
To death they rush, but rude their shock—not
    unavenged they died.

On through the camp the column trod—King
    Louis turns his rein ;
"Not yet, my liege," Saxe interposed, "the Irish
    troops remain ;"
And Fontenoy, famed Fontenoy, had been a
    Waterloo,
Were not these exiles ready then, fresh, vehement,
    and true.

IV.

"Lord Clare," he says, "you have your wish—
    there are your Saxon foes ;"
The marshal almost smiles to see, so furiously he
    goes !
How fierce the look these exiles wear, who're wont
    to be so gay !
The treasured wrongs of fifty years are in their
    hearts to-day—
The treaty broken ere the ink wherewith 'twas
    writ could dry,
Their plundered homes, their ruined shrines, their
    women's parting cry,
Their priesthood hunted down like wolves, their
    country overthrown—
Each looks as if revenge for all rested on him
    alone.
On Fontenoy, on Fontenoy, nor ever yet else-
    where,
Rushed on to fight a nobler band than these proud
    exiles were.

V.

O'Brien's voice is hoarse with joy, as, halting, he commands,
"Fix bay'nets—charge." Like mountain storms rush on these fiery bands!
Thin is the English column now, and faint their volleys grow,
Yet, must'ring all the strength they have, they make a gallant show.
They dress their ranks upon the hill to face that battle-wind—
Their bayonets the breakers' foam; like rocks, the men behind !
One volley crashes from their line, when, through the surging smoke,
With empty guns clutched in their hands, the headlong Irish broke.
On Fontenoy, on Fontenoy, hark to that fierce huzzah !
"Revenge ! remember Limerick ! dash down the Sassenach."

VI.

Like lions leaping at a fold when mad with hunger's pang,
Right up against the English line the Irish exiles sprang.
Bright was their steel, 'tis bloody now, their guns are filled with gore ;

Through shattered ranks, and severed files, and
    trampled flags they tore.
The English strove with desp'rate strength, paused,
    rallied, staggered, fled—
The green hill-side is matted close with dying and
    with dead.
Across the plain and far away passed on that
    hideous wrack,
While cavalier and fantassin dash in upon their
    track.
On Fontenoy, on Fontenoy, like eagles in the sun,
With bloody plumes the Irish stand—the field is
    fought and won !

OUR COURSE.

BY J. D. FRAZER.

We looked for guidance to the *blind !*
    We sued for counsel to the *dumb !*
Fling the vain fancy to the wind—
    Their hour is past and *ours* is come ;
They gave, in that propitious hour,
    Nor kindly look nor gracious tone ;
But heaven has not denied us pow'r
    To do their duty, and our own.

II.

And is it true that tyrants throw
    Their shafts among us steeped in gall?
And every arrow, swift or slow,
    Points foremost still, ascent or fall?
Still sure to wound us, though the aim
    Seem ta'en remotely, or amiss?
And men with spirits feel no shame
    To brook so dark a doom as this!

III.

Alas! the nobles of the land
    Are like our long-deserted halls;
No living voices, clear and grand,
    Respond when foe or freedom calls.
But ever and anon ascends
    Low moaning, when the tempest rolls—
A tone that desolation lends
    Some crevice of their ruined souls!

IV.

So be it—yet shall we prolong
    Our prayers, when deeds would serve our need?
Or wait for woes, the swift and strong
    Can ward by strength or 'scape by speed?
The vilest of the vile of earth
    Were nobler than our proud array,
If, suffering bondage from our birth,
    We will not burst it when we may.

V.

And has the bondage not been borne
  Till all our softer nature fled—
Till tyranny's dark tide had worn
  Down to the stubborn rock its bed?
But if the current, cold and deep,
  That channel through all time retain,
At worst, by heaven! it shall not sweep
  Unruffled o'er our hearts again!

VI.

Up for the land!—'tis ours—'tis ours!
  The proud man's sympathies are all
Like silvery clouds, whose faithless show'rs
  Come frozen to hailstones in their fall.
Our freedom and the sea-bird's food
  Are hid beneath deep ocean waves,
And who should search and sound the flood
  If not the sea-birds and the slaves?

THE VICTOR'S BURIAL.

BY THOMAS DAVIS.

I.

Wrap him in his banner, the best shroud of the brave —
Wrap him in his *onchu*,* and take him to his grave;
Lay him not down lowly, like a bulwark overthrown,
But gallantly upstanding, as if risen from his throne,
With his *craiseach*† in his hand, and his sword on his thigh,
With his war-belt on his waist, and his *cathbarr*‡ on high;
Put his *fleasg*§ upon his neck; his green flag round him fold,
Like ivy round a castle wall, not conquered, but grown old.
   Wirasthrue! oh, wirasthrue! oh, wirasthrue! ochone!
   Weep for him! oh, weep for him! but remember, in your moan,
     That he died in his pride,
     With his foes about him strown.

* Flag.   † Harp.   ‡ Helmet.   § Collar.

II.

Oh! shrine him in Beinn-Edair,* with his face
   towards the foe,
As an emblem that not death our defiance can lay
   low ;
Let him look across the waves from the pro-
   montory's breast,
To menace back the east, and to sentinel the west.
Sooner shall these channel waves the iron coast
   cut through,
Than the spirit he has left, yield, Easterlings! to
   you.
Let his coffin be the hill, let the eagles of the sea
Chorus with the surges round the *tuireamh*† of
   the free!
   Wirasthrue! oh, wirasthrue! oh, wirasthrue!
      ochone!
   Weep for him! oh, weep for him! but remem-
      ber, in your moan,
     That he died in his pride,
     With his foes around him strown!

    * Howth.   † A masculine lament.

BROTHERS, ARISE!

BY GEORGE PHILLIPS.

[The subjoined address was written to the Irish Nationalists, during the Monster Meetings of 1843, by one of the English Puseyites, and may be fairly taken to represent the sentiments of many of that great party. They cannot but sympathize with a people not only oppressed for conscience' sake, but for opinions differing little from their own; and it is natural that the sympathy of the young and earnest should exhibit the bold and emphatic spirit which breathes through this poem.]

I.

BROTHERS, arise! the hour has come
    To strike the blow for truth and God!
Why sit ye folded up and dumb?
    Why, bending, kiss the tyrant's rod?
Is there no hope upon the earth?
    No charter in the starry sky?
Has freedom no ennobling worth?
    And man no immortality?

II.

Ah, brothers! think ye what ye are—
    What glorious work ye have to do;
And how they wait ye near and far
    To do the same the wide world through.
The wide world sunk in dreams and death,
    With guilt and wrong upon its breast,
Like nightmares choking up its breath,
    And murdering all its holy rest!

III.

Bethink ye how, with heart and brain,
   This God-like work were ablest done;
For man must ne'er go back again
   And lose the triumphs he has won.
Ye who have spurned the tyrant's power,
   And fought your own great spirits free,
Forget not in this trying hour
   The claims of struggling slavery!

IV.

The wise and good—oh! where are they,
   To guide us onward to the right,
Untruth and specious lies to slay,
   And red oppression in its might?
Come forth, my brothers! on with us—
   Direct the battle we would give;
By thousands we would die—if thus
   The millions yet unborn may live.

V.

For what is death to him who dies
   With God's own blessing on his head?
A charter—not a sacrifice;
   A life immortal to the dead.
And life itself is only great
   When man devotes himself to be,
By virtue, thought, and deed, the mate
   Of God's own children and the free.

VI.

And are we free ? Oh ! blot and shame !
    That men who for a thousand years
Have battled on through fire and flame,
    And nourished, with their blood and tears,
Religion—freedom—civil right,
    Should tamely suffer traitor hands
To dash them into gloom and night,
    And bind their very God with bands.

VII.

And will ye bear, my brother men,
    To see your altars trampled down ?
Shall Christ's great heart bleed out again
    Beneath the scoffer's spear and frown ?
Shall priests proclaim that God is not,
    And from the devil's gospel teach
Those worldly doctrines, unforgot,
    Which burning tyrants loved to preach ?

VIII.

Shall traitors to the human right,
    To God and truth, have boundless sway,
And ye not rush into the fight
    And wrench the sacred cross away,
And tear the scrolls of freedom, bought
    With blood of martyrs and the brave,
From men who, with derisive sport,
    Defy you on the martyr's grave ?

IX.

Ah, no!—uprushing, million-strong,
   The trodden people come at last—
Their fiery souls, pent up so long,
   Burst out in flames all thick and fast;
And thunder-words and lightning-deeds
   Strike terror to the wrong, who flee,
Till, lo!—at last the wronger bleeds,
   And, dying, leaves the nation free!

WHAT'S MY THOUGHT LIKE?

BY JOHN O'CONNELL.

> "What's my thought like?"
> "How is it like?" &c.
> "What would you do with it?"
>   *Nursery Game.*

I.

WHAT'S my thought like?—What's my thought like?
      Like a column tumbled down,
Its noble shaft and capital with moss and weeds o'er-grown!
How is my thought so like unto a column thus laid low?
Because your thought is Ireland now, laid prostrate even so!

What with it would you do?—oh! say what with
    it would you do?
Upraise it from the earth again, aloft to mankind's
    view!
A sign unto all those that mourn, throughout
    earth's vast domain,
That Heaven rewards the patient, and will make
    them joy again.

II.

What's my thought like?—What's my thought
    like?
              Like a gallant ship on shore.
Dismasted all, and helpless now, amid the breakers'
    roar!
Her crew, so faithful once to her, each seeking
    plank and spar,
To 'scape from her, and safety find upon the land
    afar.
How is my thought like such poor ship in peril
    and distress?
Because your thought is Ireland now, whose peril
    is no less!
What with it would you do?—oh! say what with
    it would you do?
Like to some few but faithful hearts among the
    vessel's crew,

Stand by her to the last I would, and die, if so
    decreed,
Ere man should dare to say to me, *You failed her
    at her need!*

III.

What's my thought like?—What's my thought
    like?
                    Like a land by Nature blessed
Beyond most other lands on earth, and yet the
    most distressed;
A teeming soil, abounding streams, wide havens,
    genial air—
And yet a people ever plunged in suffering and
    care!
Eight millions of a noble race—high-minded, pure,
    and good—
Kept subject to a petty gang—a miserable brood—
Strong but in England's constant hate, and help
    to keep us down,
And blast the smiles of Nature fair with man's
    unholy frown!
How is it like my thought, again?—How is it like
    my thought?
Because your thought is Ireland's self—and even thus
    her lot!

IV.

What with it would you do, again?—what with it
    would you do?

Work even to the death I would, to rive her chain
    in two!
To help her 'gainst unnatural sons, and foreign
    foemen's rage,
And all her hapless people's woes and bitter griefs
    assuage.
Bid them be happy now, at length, in this their
    rescued land—
That land no longer marked and cursed with
    slavery's withering brand:
No longer slave to England!—but her sister, if
    she will—
Prompt to give friendly aid at need, and to forget
    all ill:
But holding high her head, and, with serenest brow,
Claiming, amid earth's nations all, her fitting
    station now!

THIS is my thought—it is your thought.—If thus
    each Irish heart
Will only think, and purpose thus henceforth to
    act its part,
Full soon their honest boast shall be—that she was
    made by them
Great, glorious, free!—the earth's first flower!—
    the ocean's brightest gem!

STEADY.

BY R. D. WILLIAMS.

"Courage—your most necessary virtue—consists not in blind resistance, but in knowing when to forbear."—THE NATION, *June* 17, 1843.

I.

STEADY! host of freedom, steady!
　Ponder, gather, watch, mature:
Tranquil be, though ever ready—
　Prompt to act and to endure.

II.

Aimless, rage you not insanely,
　Like a maniac with his chain,
Struggling madly, therefore vainly,
　And lapsing back to bonds again.

III.

But, observe, the clouds o'er Keeper
　Long collect their awful ire —
Long they swell more dark and deeper—
　When they burst, all heaven's on fire!

IV.

Freedom's bark to port is running,
　But beware the lurking shelves;
And would you conquer tyrants' cunning,
　Brethren, conquer first yourselves.

V.

Though thy cheek insulted burn—
    Though they call thee coward-slave—
Scoff nor blow shalt thou return :
    Trust me, this is *more* than brave.

VI.

Fortitude hath shackles riven,
    More than spear or flashing gun ;
Freedom, like the thrones of heaven,
    Is by suff'ring virtue won.

VII.

Though thy brother still deride thee,
    Yield thou love for foolish hate :
He'll, perhaps, ere long, beside thee,
    Proudly, boldly, share thy fate.

VIII.

Steady! steady! ranks of freedom,
    Pure and holy are our bands ;
Heaven approves, and angels lead them,
    For truth and justice are our brands.

THE FIRESIDE.

BY D. F. M'CARTHY.

I.

I HAVE tasted all life's pleasures—I have snatched
    at all its joys—
The dance's merry measures, and the revel's festive
    noise ;
Though wit flashed bright the live-long night, and
    flowed the ruby tide,
I sighed for thee—I sighed for thee, my own fire-
    side!

II.

In boyhood's dreams I wandered far across the
    ocean's breast,
In search of some bright earthly star—some happy
    isle of rest ;
I little thought the bliss I sought in roaming far
    and wide,
Was sweetly centred all in thee, my own fire-
    side !

III.

How sweet to turn at evening's close from all our
    cares away,
And end, in calm, serene repose, the swiftly pass-
    ing day !

The pleasant books, the smiling looks of sister or
 of bride,
All fairy ground doth make around one's own fireside!

IV.

"My lord" would never condescend to honor my
 poor hearth;
"His grace" would scorn a host or friend of mere
 plebeian birth;
And yet the lords of human kind whom man has
 deified
For ever meet in converse sweet around my fireside!

V.

The poet sings his deathless songs, the sage his
 lore repeats,
The patriot tells his country's wrongs, the chief his
 warlike feats;
Though far away may be their clay, and gone
 their earthly pride,
Each godlike mind, in books enshrined, still haunts
 my fireside.

VI.

Oh! let me glance a moment through the coming
 crowd of years—
Their triumphs or their failures—their sunshine or
 their tears!

How poor or great may be my fate, I care not
  what betide,
So peace and love but hallow thee, my own fireside!

VII.

Still let me hold the vision close and closer to my
  sight;
Still, still, in hopes elysian, let my spirit wing its
  flight;
Still let me dream life's shadowy stream may yield
  from out its tide
A mind at rest—a tranquil breast—a quiet fireside.

O'DONNELL ABU.

A.D. 1597.

BY M. J. M'CANN.

Proudly the note of the trumpet is sounding,
  Loudly the war-cries arise on the gale,
Fleetly the steed by Loc Suilig* is bounding
  To join the thick squadrons in Saimear's green
    vale.
      On, every mountaineer,
      Strangers to flight and fear;

* Lough Swilly.

Rush to the standard of dauntless Red Hugh !*
   Bonnought and gallowglass,†
    Throng from each mountain-pass !
On for old Erin—O'Donnell abu !

II.

Princely O'Neil to our aid is advancing,
  With many a chieftain and warrior-clan ;
A thousand proud steeds in his vanguard are prancing,
  'Neath the borderers brave from the banks of the Bann ;
    Many a heart shall quail
    Under its coat of mail ;
   Deeply the merciless foeman shall rue,
    When on his ear shall ring,
    Borne on the breeze's wing,
   Tir-Conaill's dread war-cry—O'Donnell abu !

III.

Wildly o'er Desmond the war-wolf is howling,
  Fearless the eagle sweeps over the plain,
The fox in the streets of the city is prowling—
  All, all who would scare them are banished or slain !
    Grasp, every stalwart hand,
    Hackbut and battle-brand—

---

* The famous Red Hugh O'Donnell, who aided O'Neil in defeating the best generals and most brilliant armies of Elizabeth.
† See note, page 45.

Pay them all back the deep debt so long due:
    Norris and Clifford well
    Can of Tir-Conaill tell—
Onward to glory—O'Donnell abu!

IV.

Sacred the cause that Clann-Conaill's defending—
  The altars we kneel at and homes of our sires;
Ruthless the ruin the foe is extending—
  Midnight is red with the plunderer's fires!
    On with O'Donnell, then,
    Fight the old fight again,
  Sons of Tir-Conaill, all valiant and true!
    Make the false Saxon feel
    Erin's avenging steel!
Strike for your country!—O'Donnell abu!

FILL HIGH TO-NIGHT.

BY WILLIAM MULCHINECK.

I.

Fill high to-night in your halls of light,
    The toast on our lips shall be—
"The sinewy hand, the glittering brand,
    Our homes and our altars free."

II.

Though the coward pale, like the girl, may wail
    And sleep in his chains for years,
The sound of our mirth shall pass over earth
    With balm for a nation's tears.

III.

A curse for the cold, a cup for the bold,
    A smile for the girls we love;
And for him who'd bleed in his country's need
    A home in the skies above.

IV.

We have asked the page of a former age,
    For hope secure and bright,
And the spell it gave to the stricken slave
    Was in one strong word—"Unite."

V.

Though the wind howl free o'er a simple tree
   Till it bends beneath its frown—
For many a day it will howl away
   Ere a forest be stricken down.

VI.

By the martyred dead who for freedom bled,
   By all that man deems divine,
Our patriot band for a sainted land
   Like brothers shall all combine.

VII.

Then fill to-night in our halls of light,
   The toast on our lips must be—
" The sinewy hand, the glittering brand,
   Our homes and our altars free."

THE SLAVES' BILL.

BY WILLIAM DRENNAN.

I.

Aye, brand our arms, nor them alone,
   But brand our brows, degraded race—
Oh! how a fear can England own
   Of men who cannot feel disgrace?

Men! *Are* we men? We talk as such—
　　Heavens! how we talk! but—vain alarms!
Nought masculine endures so much :
　　Then brand our brows as well as arms.

II.

This brand is not an ugly thing—
　　May seem an ornament, indeed ;
The shame to some would be the sting,
　　But not to slaves who dare not bleed !
Six hundred weary years have passed,
　　And which without some newer harms
From dear Old England? This, the last,
　　Is *but an insult*—brand our arms !

III.

Yes, brand our language, faith, and name !
　　Black down time's river let them roll ;
Let Erin be a word of shame,
　　And burn its mem'ry from my soul !
O Erin ! Erin ! nevermore
　　That darling name let me repeat ;
If such the sons my mother bore,
　　West-Britain were a sound as sweet.

IV.

Aye, brand us all ! yet still we crave
　　A pittance at our master's door :
Then leave the wealthy Irish slave
　　His bottle, club, and paramour !

And leave the wretched serf his wife—
    (You may—she has not many charms)—
Potatoes, and his paltry life;
    But leave us not ev'n branded arms!

V.

Mad as ye are, who reckless dare
    To mock the spirit God hath given,
Pause, ere you drive us in despair
    To its appeal—from man to heaven!
From calmer eyes the furies glare,
    And colder bosoms vengeance warms,
Till rage finds weapons, ev'rywhere,
    For Nature's two unbranded arms!

THE LAMENT OF *GRAINNE MAOL!**

BY HUGH HARKIN.

I.

John Bull was a *bodach*, as rich as a Jew;
As griping, as grinding, as conscienceless too;
A wheedler, a shuffler, a rogue by wholesale,
And a swindler, moreover, says GRAINNE MAOL!

II.

John Bull was a banker, both pursy and fat,
With gold in his pockets, and plenty of that;
And he tempted his neighbors to sell their entail—
Tis by scheming he prospers, says GRAINNE MAOL!

III.

John Bull was a farmer, with cottiers galore—
Stout "chawbacons" once, that like bullocks could roar;
Hard work and low wages and Peel's sliding scale
Have bothered their courage, says GRAINNE MAOL!

* Vulgarly written, but rightly pronounced, "Grann Wail."

IV.

John Bull was a bruiser, so sturdy and stout,
A boisterous bully—at bottom a clout—
For when you squared up he was apt to turn tail—
Brother Jonathan lashed him, says GRAINNE MAOL!

V.

John Bull was a merchant, and many his ships,
His harbors, his dock-yards, and big building slips;
And the ocean he claimed as his rightful entail—
Monsieur Parley-vouz *bars that*, says GRAINNE MAOL!

VI.

John Bull had dependencies, many and great—
Fine, fertile, and fat—every one an estate;
But he pilfered and plundered wholesale and retail—
There's Canada, sign's on it, says GRAINNE MAOL!

VII.

John Bull! was a saint in the western clime,
Stood fast for the truths of the Gospel sublime,
Vowed no other faith in the end could avail;
Is't the Jugghernaut champion? says GRAINNE MAOL!

VIII.

John Bull had a sister, so fair to be seen,
With a blush like a rose, and a mantle of green,
And a soft, swelling bosom!—On hill or in dale,
Oh! where could you fellow sweet GRAINNE
　MAOL?

IX.

And John loved his sister, without e'er a flam,
Like the fox and the pullet, the wolf and the
　lamb;
So he paid her a visit—but mark her bewail:
My title deed's vanished! says GRAINNE
　MAOL!

X.

Then he rummaged her commerce and ravaged her
　plains;
Razed her churches and castles—her children in
　chains,
With pitch-caps, triangles, and gibbets wholesale,
Betokened John's love to poor GRAINNE MAOL!

XI.

But one of her children, more *bould* than the rest,
Took it into his head for to make a *request!*
Our rights, Uncle John! Else our flag on the gale!
Faix, he got an instalment, says GRAINNE
　MAOL!

XII.

And now he is at the *Ould Growler* again,
With his logic, and law, and—*three millions of men!*
And nothing will plaise him, just now, but REPALE,
"*Mo seact n-anam aslig tu,*"* says GRAINNE
   MAOL!

XIII.

But should John turn gruff, and decline the de-
   mand,
What means of success may be at our command,
Although he be humbled, and now getting frail?
My "NATION" will tell you, says GRAINNE
   MAOL!

XIV.

(*"NATION" LOQUITUR.*)
" If, stubborn and wilful, he still should refuse
To hear our just claims, or submit to our views,
And resolve, in his folly, to hold the 'entail,'
We'll '*kick his Dumbarton*' for GRAINNE MAOL!"

---

* "Seven times as dear as the soul within me."

LOVE'S LONGINGS.

BY THOMAS DAVIS.

I.

To the conqueror his crowning.
    First freedom to the slave,
And air unto the drowning
    Sunk in the ocean's wave,
And succor to the faithful
    Who fight their flag above,
Are sweet, but far less grateful
    Than were my lady's love.

II.

I know I am not worthy
    Of one so young and bright;
And yet I would do for thee
    Far more than others might:
I cannot give you pomp or gold
    If you should be my wife,
But I can give you love untold,
    And true in death or life.

III.

Methinks that there are passions
    Within that heaving breast,
To scorn their heartless fashions,
    And wed whom you love best.

Methinks you would be prouder
    As the struggling patriot's bride,
Than if rank your home should crowd, or
    Cold riches round you glide.

IV.

Oh! the watcher longs for morning,
    And the infant cries for light,
And the saint for heaven's warning,
    And the vanquished pray for might;
But their prayer when lowest kneeling,
    And their suppliance most true,
Are cold to the appealing
    Of this longing heart to you.

PAST AND PRESENT.

["Where are the monster meetings—the myriads of Tara and Mullaghmast?"—*English Press passim.*]

I.

Where are the marshalled hosts that met
　Last year the island over?
Here are they, calm, but ready yet,
　Like warriors couched in cover;
With zeal as ardent, rage as deep,
　As bitter wrongs to feed them;
As stalwart limbs—let fools go sleep,
　And dream of stifled freedom.

II.

A lull—the tempest lulls, and then
　The blast the forest scatters;
The thunder peals are stilled—again
　The bolt the turret shatters;
And low the brandished hatchet sings
　For mightier stroke uplifted—
Round, round it swings, then down it rings,
　And toughest blocks are rifted.

III.

There is a sullen under-hum
　Will swell to a tornado;
A day shall come will render dumb
　Our English lords' bravado—

When Irish parties, hand in hand,
    And shoulder up to shoulder,
Shall take their stand on Irish land,
    And buried feuds shall moulder.

IV.

Who chafes or falters at delay,
    Faint-hearted and short-seeing?
What is it all?—a winter's day
    'Mid ages of ill-being.
Ah! thus our fathers were undone!
    They sickened and seceded—
Had they but battled constant on,
    Our battle were not needed.

V.

God knows his times: one thing know we—
    Our ills, and what will end them;
That these our fetters loosed must be,
    Or should we file or rend them?
Shall we sit looking at our gyves,
    Who talked so loud a year hence?
Shall we, who frankly staked our lives,
    Grudge earnest perseverance?

VI.

We'll hoard our might and gather more—
    We'll draw our brothers nigh us—

We'll give our minds, from wisdom's store,
  A firmer, manlier bias—
We'll rouse the nation near and far,
  From Rathlin to Cean-mara,
Then show them where the masses are
  Of Mullaghmast and Tara.

SLIABH CUILINN.

THE ARMS OF "EIGHTY-TWO."

BY M. J. BARRY.

I.

THEY rose to guard their fatherland—
  In stern resolve they rose,
In bearing firm, in purpose grand,
  To meet the world as foes.
They rose, as brave men ever do;
    And, flashing bright,
    They bore to light
The Arms of "Eighty-two!"

II.

Oh! 'twas a proud and solemn sight
  To mark that broad array
Come forth to claim a nation's right
  'Gainst all who dared gainsay;

And despots shrunk, appalled to view
    The men who bore,
    From shore to shore,
The Arms of " Eighty-two !"

III.

They won her right—they passed away—
    Within the tomb they rest—
And coldly lies the mournful clay
    Above each manly breast;
But Ireland still may proudly view
    What that great host
    Had cherished most—
The Arms of " Eighty-two !"

IV.

Time-honored comrades of the brave—
    Fond relics of their fame !
Does Ireland hold one coward slave
    Would yield you up to shame?
One dastard who would tamely view
    The alien's hand,
    Insulting, brand
The Arms of " Eighty-two ?"

THE WEXFORD MASSACRE.
1649.
BY M. J. BARRY.

I.

They knelt around the Cross divine—
    The matron and the maid;
They bowed before redemption's sign,
    And fervently they prayed:
Three hundred fair and helpless ones,
    Whose crime was this alone—
Their valiant husbands, sires, and sons,
    Had battled for their own.

II.

Had battled bravely, but in vain—
    The Saxon won the fight,
And Irish corses strewed the plain
    Where Valor slept with Right.
And now that man of demon guilt
    To fated Wexford flew—
The red blood reeking on his hilt,
    Of hearts to Erin true!

III.

He found them there—the young, the old,
    The maiden, and the wife:
Their guardian brave in death were cold,
    Who dared for *them* the strife.

They prayed for mercy—God on high!
   Before *thy* cross they prayed,
And ruthless Cromwell bade them die
   To glut the Saxon blade!

IV.

Three hundred fell—the stifled prayer
   Was quenched in woman's blood;
Nor youth nor age could move to spare
   From slaughter's crimson flood.
But nations keep a stern account
   Of deeds that tyrants do;
And guiltless blood to Heaven will mount,
   And Heaven avenge it, too!

THE ANTI-IRISH IRISHMAN.

BY HUGH HARKIN.

I.

FROM polar seas to torrid climes,
   Where'er the trace of man is found,
What common feeling marks our kind,
   And sanctifies each spot of ground?
What virtue in the human heart
   The proudest tribute can command?
The dearest, purest, holiest, best,
   The lasting love of FATHERLAND!

II.

Then who's the wretch that basely spurns
   The ties of country, kindred, friends—
That barters every nobler aim
   For sordid views—for private ends?
One slave alone on earth you'll find
   Through Nature's universal span,
So lost to virtue, dead to shame—
   The anti-Irish Irishman.

III.

Our fields are fertile, rich our floods,
   Our mountains bold, majestic, grand;
Our air is balm, and every breeze
   Wings health around our native land.
But who despises all her charms,
   And mocks her gifts where'er he can?
Why, he, the Norman's sneaking slave,
   The anti-Irish Irishman.

IV.

The Norman—spawn of fraud and guile—
   Ambitious sought our peaceful shore,
And, leagued with native guilt, despoiled
   And deluged Erin's fields with gore!
Who gave the foeman footing here?
   What wretch unholy led her van?
The prototype of modern slave,
   An anti Irish Irishman!

V.

For ages rapine ruled our plains,
    And slaughter raised "his red right hand,"
And virgins shrieked, and roof-trees blazed,
    And desolation swept the land!
And who would not those ills arrest,
    Or aid the patriotic plan
To burst his country's galling chains?
    The anti-Irish Irishman.

VI.

But now, too great for fetters grown,
    Too proud to bend a slavish knee,
Loved Erin mocks the tyrant's thrall,
    And firmly vows she shall be free!
But mark yon treacherous, stealthy knave,
    That bends beneath his country's ban!
Let infamy eternal brand
    That anti-Irish Irishman.

THE END.

www.ingramcontent.com/pod-product-compliance
Lightning Source LLC
Chambersburg PA
CBHW031728230426
43669CB00007B/286